Prais

OKAYEST MOM

"Natalie's journey will touch and inspire you. As an adoptive mother I hear the label often. But it's not okayest; it is real. Are you their 'real mom'? This book will make those words catch in your throat. This is the stuff that turns a woman into a real mom."
—Jami Amerine of the blog *Sacred Ground, Sticky Floors* and author of *Stolen Jesus*

"Heartfelt, encouraging, and power-packed. Natalie's book will give clarity to so many people and encourage them to think about family in a whole new way."
—Havilah Cunnington, bestselling author of *Eat Pray Hustle* and *Stronger than the Struggle*

OKAYEST MOM

When God's Plan of Adoption Doubled My Family

NATALIE GWYN

New York   Nashville

FaithWords

Hachette Book Group

1290 Avenue of the Americas, New York, NY 10104

faithwords.com

twitter.com/faithwords

First edition: June 2018

FaithWords is a division of Hachette Book Group, Inc. The FaithWords name and logo are trademarks of Hachette Book Group, Inc.

The publisher is not responsible for websites (or their content) that are not owned by the publisher.

The Hachette Speakers Bureau provides a wide range of authors for speaking events. To find out more, go to www.hachettespeakersbureau.com or call (866) 376-6591.

All Scripture quotations, unless otherwise indicated, are taken from THE MESSAGE, copyright © 1993, 1994, 1995, 1996, 2000, 2001, 2002. Used by permission of NavPress Publishing Group.

Scripture quotations marked NASB are taken from the NEW AMERICAN STANDARD BIBLE®, copyright © 1960, 1962, 1963, 1968, 1971, 1972, 1973, 1975, 1977, 1995 by The Lockman Foundation. Used by permission. (www.Lockman.org).

Scripture quotations marked NLT are taken from the Holy Bible, New Living Translaton, copyright © 1996, 2004. Used by permission of Tyndale House Publishers, Inc., Wheaton Illinois 60189, U.S.A. All rights reserved.

In chapter 7, the lullaby "Kisses in the Wind," copyright 1997 by Pamela Durkota.

Library of Congress Cataloging-in-Publication Data has been applied for.

ISBNs: 978-1-4789-9248-6 (trade paperback); 978-1-4789-9249-3 (ebook)

Printed in the United States of America

LSC-C

10 9 8 7 6 5 4 3 2 1

CONTENTS

FOREWORD

When my wife, Sara, and I were first considering adopting four sisters from Ethiopia (ages 5, 8, 12, and 15) we were trying to meet and get advice from those who had already walked that road. It can be hard to connect with an adoptive family that has taken on the challenge of adopting four older children all at the same time, so we were both surprised and excited that in our small town of Redding, California, there was a family that had done the very same thing we were considering. Anytime you face a big challenge in life you want to pick the minds of those who are living out and through the challenge. Talking with Natalie prior to our adoption decision really helped us to decide to adopt our four daughters.

What I still remember from our initial meeting with Natalie was how real she was. She shared all the good things that came with adoption and all the challenges along the way. Natalie is a very authentic, relatable, loving, enthusiastic, and vibrant adoptive mother. I could have listened to her stories and advice for days, as I was so hungry to learn from her experiences. What I remember the most from our meeting was her commenting that, without a doubt, it is worth it and she would do it all over again. To have someone who has been to the top of the mountain tell you that the journey is worth taking is all we needed to hear to begin our own journey. Now, we have had our four daughters home for over a year and have become close friends with the Putnams. We continue to learn from them and be inspired by their lives to this day.

If you are at all interested in adoption and want a fun yet informative and encouraging read on the subject, I strongly encourage you to dive into Natalie's book. You are sure to be encouraged, strengthened and prepared for whatever challenges lie in front of you.

—Ryan Hall, professional runner, Olympian, U.S. record holder in the half marathon, speaker, author of *Running with Joy*, and adoptive father

OKAYEST
MOM

1

STICKY

No! I no eat! I no like this!" my daughter yelled in her broken English.

Overwhelmed by the chaos around me, I stood in my pajamas and cried. My counters were sticky with syrup. A glass lay on its side, slowly dripping milk onto the floor. My children were arguing. One daughter was crying. Another glared in defiance.

It was not even eight in the morning, and I was tired. Tired of all the mess. Tired of the emotional drain. Tired of the needs surrounding me. Who were these children? Why did they ask so much of me? How had I ended up here? *God, why did You think I could do this? Are You sure You chose the right woman for the job? I don't think I was cut out to be a mom to these six children. It's too hard.*

On paper, I certainly wasn't the best applicant. My résumé included the character qualities of "selfish" and "impatient." My work history stated: "Plotted her own course through life. Self-sufficient. Doesn't need to rely on others to get the job done."

But God skipped over those qualifications and focused on the small print. He looked at me and saw instead "loving," "joyful," and "resilient." And most important, He saw the quality He seeks in every applicant for every task He has called us to. He looked at me and saw "willing." That was all it took.

He assigned me to be a mother to these six children, and with that and one signature from a judge in Ethiopia, my life was changed forever. Seemingly overnight, I had gone from having two children, who began their lives in my womb, to six, four of whom were born in a rural hut in Ethiopia and did not yet speak English. Six children with such different histories, now part of the same family. Six children who needed me to love them, even if I didn't always feel loving.

We had been together as a family for only a few weeks. It was not going well.

I somehow had to raise these children. Educate all six. I had to teach my new children English, the alphabet, and how to read. I also had to teach them how to use indoor plumbing and the value of toilet paper, but maybe I would leave that for tomorrow.

I turned my back to the disaster and reached for my phone. I had an incoming text from my friends. My dear, sweet, encouraging friends. They were inviting me to join their Bible study. They met every Thursday morning from nine to eleven and were working their way through the book of Matthew. Would I like to join them?

Their few words spelled out how drastically my life had changed. Tears and resentment overflowed as I realized I would have no more Thursday morning Bible studies. No more coffee dates. No more girls' nights out. My time was not my own. My life was not my own. For the foreseeable future, my life belonged to these children. These children who needed me more than they would admit. They needed a mother to be close, even when they pushed away with their words and actions. God had entrusted these six children to my care.

What in the world was He thinking?

As I stood surrounded by sticky countertops and defiant children, reading those words that signaled an end to my old life, I felt God remind me that my life is not my own. I belong to Him. In the years to come He would have to remind me of this over and over again as I began a daily, sometimes hourly practice of putting aside my own desires to run the race set before me.

Late in the book of Acts, Paul bade good-bye to his friends in Ephesus as he followed God's leading and stepped into a new ministry. Although he knew God was calling him to Jerusalem, he had no idea what the journey might hold:

But there is another urgency before me now. I feel compelled to go to Jerusalem. I'm completely in the dark about what will happen when I get there. I do know that it won't be any picnic, for the Holy Spirit has let me know repeatedly and clearly that there are hard times and imprisonment ahead. But that matters little. What matters most to me is to finish what God started: the job the Master Jesus gave me of letting everyone I meet know all about this incredibly extravagant generosity of God. (Acts 20:22–24)

I knew what God was calling me to. He was calling me to be a mother. More specifically, He was calling me to be a mother to these six children. These six very special children He had given me.

But I didn't know how to do that. I didn't know how to meet each of their specific needs, how to help them heal from their traumas, how to navigate the tricky waters of loving biological children and adopted children in ways that would make them all feel equal and valued and worthy.

I didn't know how to create a family out of the chaos. I empathized with Paul when he said he was "completely in the dark about what will happen when I get there. I do know that it won't be any picnic."

For me, it surely wasn't going to be a picnic. That morning in my kitchen was the tip of the iceberg. We had been home for only a few weeks. We were still enjoying the honeymoon phase of our adoption.

That honeymoon was delightful while it lasted. Everyone was on their best behavior, and the novelty of being a family of eight was enough to temper my exhaustion. We had not yet encountered the rages that would last for hours, the words screamed in anger that cut to the heart. We had heard none of the shouts of "I hate you" and "I want to die" that would pepper later conversations. My husband and I were a team. Our daughter had not yet driven a wedge between us as she tried to pit us against each other in her battle for emotional control.

Yet I could feel the storm brewing. As I stood in my sun-dappled kitchen, I could feel spiritual forces at work. Darkness creeping in around the edges. Battles were taking place for the ownership of hearts. Little did I know those battles would become all-consuming as we fought for the future of our children.

Wouldn't it have been easier to confine my obedience to God to areas that would not so drastically affect my family?

Yes.

It would have been easier. But it would not have been better.

Adoption is a thief. It robs children of their past. It robs families of their legacy. It robs hearts of their security. It robbed me of so many firsts.

I missed my children's first words. I missed their first steps. I missed their wrinkly, milky infant newness. I don't know what my children looked like before the age of five. We have no baby pictures. All of that is lost to another time and another woman. Their past belongs to her. Their future belongs to God.

Adoption is also a beautiful benefactress, bestowing gifts when you least expect them. It gives you a new perspective on everything around you. A new appreciation for the moments that might never have been. A newfound understanding of love and family. I found myself watching my children with fresh eyes, noticing the details that before had swept by in a blurry haste. And I was given other firsts, different kinds of firsts, to hold on to.

The first time my children saw the ocean. The first time they said "I love you." The first time they reached out to hug me.

The first time they rode an escalator. On our flight home from Ethiopia, we had a layover in Germany. We deplaned, eager to stretch our legs. The airport in Berlin was the largest building our children had ever seen. It stretched around them, all gleaming chrome and clean, smooth floors. We walked the mostly empty corridors at two o'clock in the morning and enjoyed the wonderment on our children's faces.

As we turned a corner, an escalator appeared in front of us. It rose only one story high, but to our children it looked like it went on forever. They stood at the bottom, heads tilted back, mesmerized by the moving stairs.

I went first, stepping onto the bottom stair and allowing it to lift me higher. I turned and waved at my family, gathered around the bottom and watching me rise. When I got to the top I turned around and rode the down escalator, watching my children laugh and point.

It was their turn. We held their hands and helped them onto the moving stairs. They were unsure, one hand gripping ours, one hand gripping the railing. But they did it, rising slowly to the second floor.

Except my middle daughter. She stood firmly planted at the bottom, watching everyone else ascend.

We rode back down to her and tried to coax her into joining us. She refused, watching as we rode the escalators up and down several more times. Finally, she gathered up the courage to try it herself.

She spread her arms wide, grabbed on to the moving railings, and didn't let go. The railings slowly pulled her forward, but she left her feet stuck to the ground until she was doubled almost in half. When she couldn't bend any farther, her death grip on the railings slid her feet forward just enough to land on the bottom step. She stayed in this position, bent from the waist, butt in the air, chin tucked to her chest, as she rode that escalator all the way to the top.

In the same German airport, after we rode the escalator far too many times, we took a bathroom break. The girls each went into their stalls. As I stood washing my hands I heard the toilets flush. Then I heard shrieks.

"Mom! See! Mom!"

My daughter opened her stall door and pointed excitedly at the toilet. Then, fully clothed, she sat down on the toilet seat.

"See, Mom!" she said as she stood up quickly.

The toilet flushed. She shrieked and pointed. I laughed.

She did it again. And again. I stood in that German bathroom and watched my daughter play with the automatic toilet. These precious firsts brought laughter and a joy that would help sustain me during the hard times.

God never promised us easy. But He did promise us beauty from ashes. He did promise us blessings overflowing: "God can pour on the blessings in astonishing ways so that you're ready for anything and everything, more than just ready to do what needs to be done" (2 Cor. 9:8).

In the years to come, God's blessings would take many forms. Blessings in the form of hardship. Blessings in the forms of battles fought and demons overcome. Blessings in the forms of trials, storms, and tears. The tears were needed to wash away old wounds. The storms were needed to clear out the debris in our hearts. Through it all, I would learn to hold tight to His promise that He would make me ready to do what needed to be done.

I would not have to rely on my own strength. I did not have to count on my own understanding. He promised me strength for today and bright hope for tomorrow.

No, my life is not my own. For that I am thankful. If my life were my own, I would never have found the family God had planned for me.

2

SHUKRIYA MEANS "PEACE"

Ethiopia, 2011

Shukriya opened her eyes to the dim morning light. The sun had not yet cast its blanket of heat over the dusty fields. As she lay on the hard ground, she pulled her single cover more tightly around her and enjoyed the last remnants of the cool night air. She heard her mother stirring and rolled over to face her.

She could barely make out her mother's form bent over the pile of baskets in the corner. The only light in their hut came through the cracks in the mud walls. In the early morning hours, she had to strain to see anything. She felt, more than saw, the shadows of her brothers and sister as they lay sleeping on the floor beside her.

Faint wisps of smoke rose from the fire in the corner and escaped through the straw and branches that formed their roof. Shukriya's mother hummed softly as she readied herself for the day. Soon she would be calling her name, rousing her from her bed to help with the morning chores.

Shukriya breathed a prayer in the darkness.

Good morning, God. Will You stay with me today? I need You here with me so I am not alone. Help me to not be afraid.

Shukriya did not like being left in charge every day when her mother left. She much preferred having her older sister to rely on, but since Hamdiya had started working alongside their mother, it fell to Shukriya to care for her little brothers.

She knew her mother and sister had to work so their family could eat, but she felt lonely when they were gone. And she hated that her mother locked them inside. She said it was to keep her children safe, but it made Shukriya feel trapped.

"Shukriya." Her mother's voice cut through the darkness. "Time to get up. The fire needs to be tended, and you need to go get the water for today."

Shukriya left the warmth of her blanket and stepped over her sleeping brothers. Little Eyob, barely more than a baby, lay curled into the warmth of his brother's back. She tried not to disturb them as she arranged her scarf over her dark curls.

She picked up the large yellow water container from its place near the door and stepped outside. Shukriya never minded the walk to the river in the early morning. The sky was painted pink by the rising sun, and the fields of corn all around her turned to gold. The birds whistled as they flew overhead, and Shukriya smiled at the picture they made against the clouds.

"Thank You, God, for the birds," Shukriya prayed out loud. "They make me smile. And thank You that we have enough shiro and injera for lunch today. I won't have to worry about Eyob and Eba crying about being hungry. Thank You that the river is full so we can have enough water to drink."

Shukriya liked talking to God as she followed the path to the river. It made her feel happy inside. She wasn't sure who God was, but she imagined Him to be kind and loving. She had heard about God from the pastor at church. Much of what he said was confusing. She didn't understand why God was so different from Allah. Yet she knew that He was. Most of her neighbors were Muslim and talked about how great Allah was. But Shukriya rather preferred the God their pastor talked about. He sounded like a God who would watch over her. She liked the idea of a God who was with her all the time.

At the bank of the river, Shukriya set down her jug. She tipped it on its side and let it fill slowly. She watched for just the right moment to pull it from the river. She wanted enough water to last them all day, but not so much that she couldn't carry it home.

Struggling to lift the heavy container, she balanced the bright jug on her head as she straightened. Her family wasn't rich enough to have a donkey, but Shukriya liked to imagine they were. How nice it would be to allow the animal to carry the heavy burden. The pastor had told a story about God riding on a donkey. She liked to imagine God doing the same kinds of things she did. But she doubted He ever had to carry water if He had a donkey.

Some families could afford a donkey, but Shukriya knew hers would never be one of them. Some people had enough money for extras like animals and schooling. Some families had food every day. Maybe her family would, too, if her father were still around.

After he had gotten sick, things got harder. Her mother was doing the best she could, but sometimes at night Shukriya could hear her crying. The other day her mother had talked about sending Hamdiya away to work in a bigger city. She worried about what that might mean. First her dad had gotten sick, then their family had to move from their farm to a tiny hut. Now they barely had enough to eat.

What would happen to her? It scared her, sometimes, when she thought about the future. Hers seemed to hold only pain.

Shukriya sighed as she climbed the riverbank. She did not like to complain, so she silently moved toward home. By the time she arrived, the ache in her lower back had begun. She knew it would grow worse for the rest of the day.

She placed the water inside the door and moved toward the fire. Her brothers were awake, Eyob sitting quietly in the corner playing with a corn husk, and Eba scooping peanuts into a basket.

"You are just in time," her mother said. "If I don't hurry, all the best spots will be taken and I won't sell any peanuts today."

Her mother gathered up the baskets of peanuts, the blanket she used to mark her space on the roadside, and one roll of injera for her lunch. She hurried Hamdiya out the door in front of her.

"Good-bye, children. Obey Shukriya while I am gone. Wudahalo." (*Wudahalo* is Amharic for "I love you.")

Then she closed the door, plunging the hut into darkness. Shukriya knew their eyes would soon adjust. By midday the sun would be high enough that she could see the food she prepared for their only meal of the day.

Shukriya heard her mother drop the heavy bar across the door and the jangling of keys as the padlock was secured. She felt a stab of fear. Once again they were locked inside. Alone.

Then she remembered God. The pastor had said God was always with her.

Thank You for being here with me, God. Thank You for always being with me no matter where I go.

As Shukriya talked to God, she could feel how much He loved her. She did not know much about this God, but she loved Him all the same. She knew He would stay with her no matter where she went. Knowing He was there with her in the midst of the darkness, she felt peace.

3

BROKEN PLANS, BROKEN PEOPLE

Before I sat down to write today, I looked over my to-do list. Tuesday: Bible time, reschedule doctor's appointment, write 500 words, edit blog post, put together playlist for spin class, prep dinner. Now, I prep dinner every single day of my life. It is a task not easily forgotten. And yet I still add it to my to-do list.

I have extraordinary list-making skills. I can write a list with the best of them. And do you know where I really shine? Crossing those tasks off my list by the end of the day. Laundry? Check. Email children's teachers? Check. Make doctor's appointment? Check. Prep dinner? Check.

I find great satisfaction in those check marks. The more lists, the better: to-do lists; honey-do lists (my husband really likes my keeping him on track); Saturday chore lists (my children look forward to these all week). And I'd sooner die than grocery shop on the fly.

Every Sunday I write my week's grocery list. I'm sorry, Pastor Bill, but it seems the best place to do this is in the sanctuary. I'm listening to you preach; really, I am. But when the Holy Spirit reminds me to buy milk and shredded cheese, I have to obey His prompting and write it down. During your sermon on grace, I was inspired to buy ingredients for mango chicken curry.

Once my list is complete, I'm ready for my weekly trip to the budget grocery store. If you're looking for me at 10:30 on a Monday morning, I'll be at WinCo. Every single Monday. It's part of my weekly plan. Plan-making is also one of my strengths.

I could teach a master class on making lists. I'm addicted to them. I've not always been that way. I don't remember being a list-maker in elementary school. Planning playdates and filling in my calendar wasn't high on my priorities then. This addiction is one of many results of my childhood pain.

My memories from elementary school are admittedly vague. I have a vivid mental picture of our family's Irish setter, silky ears hanging low, tongue lolling, sitting on the front porch in the sunshine. I can picture the daisies that grew in the field behind our house. In my mind I walk through the sliding glass door into the backyard, and I am instantly surrounded by white flowers, all nodding their heads in the wind. I see myself eating watermelon on a wooden deck, wearing not a stitch of clothing, sticky red juice making rivulets down my round belly.

I especially remember my fifth-grade teacher. Mrs. Surroze planted in my heart a love for words. She taught me to read simply for the pleasure, to sit in silence and let the stories come alive with pictures and colors on the life-size screen in my mind.

I can picture the skirt my mother helped me to sew that year. Pink and covered in a tiny floral print, longer than was strictly necessary, slightly crooked at the hem, but in my mind absolutely beautiful. I remember the night our family snuck into the community pool after closing time, giggling our way through the dark as we followed our father through the summer heat.

And I remember standing outside a McDonald's, squeezing tightly the handrail that led to the doorway, scuffing my toes in the dirt along the edge of the parking lot and willing myself not to cry as my parents told us they were getting a divorce. I cried anyway. To this day I cry at the most inopportune times. Especially when I hope to hide my deep hurt, the tears seem to come of their own volition.

I cried as my parents tried to decorate the ugly reality of our newly broken family with all the pretty words they thought I needed to hear. I can still smell the smoke from the hamburgers being readied for the lunch crowd. I can see the faded blue dress I wore. I can feel the sunshine on my hair and the storm in my heart.

Although both parents eventually remarried, and I was loved and cared for, my broken family provided the framework for the rest of my childhood. Weekdays in one home, weekends in another. Alternating Christmas and Thanksgiving. Feeling the pull to love everyone equally. And always monitoring my words so I would not say anything to one parent about the other.

My siblings and I divided our time between homes. We quickly learned to adapt to our environment. *Here* we are quiet and orderly and have a bit of spending money. *Here* we are loud and laugh a lot and sometimes don't have quite enough to eat. *Here* we get lollipops and lemonade. *Here* we search the couch cushions for enough change to pay for entrance to the summer swimming pool. It was not ideal, this new lifestyle of shifting between homes and expectations and personalities.

This childhood, though I did not know it until years later, would give me an insight into my children's brokenness. My children and I, we all come from broken families. And we have all, to varying degrees, experienced restoration.

The turmoil of my elementary years gave me a great love for order. My list-making, my desire to exert control, appeared in my junior high years. It was a symptom of a heart condition, my desire for security. I thought if I was organized enough, if I had enough plans in place, I could control my future.

I began making plans for high school (AP classes with an eye toward college); college (small Christian university with an eye toward a teaching credential); career (elementary teacher until I had children of my own, then I'd become a homemaker); and relationships (date only good boys who love the Lord and find someone who wants to get married young).

My plans included sunshine, smooth sailing, and really good hair days. They included a husband, 2.5 children, and a golden retriever. I wanted to serve God with my life, but I figured I could squeeze in my ministry between the hours of nine and five and would have plenty of time left over to hang out with my friends. I wanted to live my life for Him as long as it wasn't too dirty, tiring, or radical. As long as it didn't interfere with my plans.

Instead, God offered me something better. He offered me something so all-consuming, it burned away the chaff in my heart. He offered me something so heavy, it required me to lay down my idols—the idol of security, the idol of family, and the idol of happiness—so my hands would be free to hold His gift. He offered me the opportunity to be a mother to six beautiful children.

Nothing messes with your plans and to-do lists more than being a mother, which has taught me my life is not my own. Some days my life seems to belong to my children: helping with their school-work, mediating their disagreements, listening to their stories, wiping their bottoms. My mornings are filled with cleaning spilled milk and tying shoes, packing lunch boxes and smoothing stray curls. My evenings are consumed with dinnertime, bathtime, and bedtime. And the words! The sheer quantity of words from my children's mouths is enough to bury any shred of my sanity.

For twenty minutes every afternoon I like to play the quiet game. The winner gets a sticker—and a mother who's not on the verge of a nervous break-down. Still, there's always the task of managing six children's athletic practices, counseling and medical and dental appointments, dance classes, piano lessons, and social engagements. That would be a challenge for even the most organized of people. I like to think of myself as among the most organized, but sometimes their schedules prove me wrong.

Other days my life seems to belong to my house-hold responsibilities: paying bills, meal prep, doing laundry, and ironing my husband's collared shirts. (Okay, I never iron. I hate ironing. But I buy him wrinkle-free button-downs so he leaves the house looking pressed.) Then there's my work in reading groups and teaching spin classes. Plus grocery shop-ping. And answering emails. You get the idea.

Many days it seems my life belongs to trauma.

When I'm stuck cleaning up the messes made by others. When our home's emotional thermostat falls under the control of past circumstances and I'm exhausted from the undercurrents swirling around me.

I think of the day the doctor tried to examine my child while I held down her flailing arms, somewhere between a hug and a restraint, as she screamed in fear. Or the day I reached out to hug my son and he flinched, instinctively protecting his head from the blows he expected. Or the day I dropped my daughter off for her weekly counseling appointment. I was running late and I had a carful of children.

"Honey, I will pull up to the curb and let you out. Can you walk in by yourself?"

"Yeah," she said with one shoulder shrugging, a typical response to any request these days.

"Okay. I will wait until you get inside before I leave. I'll be back in one hour."

My daughter walked away from the car sullenly, never happy to be forced into the counselor's office. When she disappeared inside the double glass doors, I pulled away.

One hour later I returned, my car now empty. I had delivered the other children to their various activities and made it back in plenty of time. I parked and walked inside the building.

The lobby was dim, the receptionist's desk empty. I looked around, confused. Where was everyone?

Then I saw my daughter's feet. They were barely visible behind the wall of chairs lining the waiting room.

"Honey?" I said. "What are you doing?"

My daughter slowly inched her way out into the room. Her face crumpled as soon as she saw me. She started crying.

I reached down and pulled her up from the floor into my arms.

"What is wrong? What were you doing back there?"

"No one was here, Mom," she said. "I sat in the chair and waited and waited, but no one was here. Then I started to worry that something bad had happened to everyone. I thought I should hide. I crawled behind the chairs so no one could see me. I had a bag of trail mix and I knew I could make that last for at least a day. But then what?"

It seemed I had missed the memo about the counselor's week of vacation. My daughter waited in an empty building for her mother to come back. Her survival instincts kicked in and she figured out how to best protect herself.

Her tears quickly turned to anger. "You left me here alone! You don't care about me at all!" she yelled as she stormed out the door toward the car.

I sighed and followed her. I had made a mistake, and I knew I would pay for it with hours, maybe days, of raging and bitterness.

Yet there are many days when my life belongs to such tender sweetness. Days I find myself, in the midst of uncertainty, overwhelmed by God's grace. Days when my daughter reaches out to hold my hand. When my son runs to greet me at the end of the school day. When I hear "I love you" from a child I thought would never say those words.

My life is not my own. Ultimately, it belongs to God. He bought me; I am His. "Or didn't you realize that your body is a sacred place, the place of the Holy Spirit? Don't you see that you can't live however you please, squandering what God paid such a high price for?" (1 Cor. 6:19–20).

Belonging to the King of the universe is a privilege and a responsibility. The life to which He has called me is nothing I ever could have imagined.

4

I LIKE BIG BUTS

When I was in school, one of my teachers posed the question "If you could ask God for one thing, what would it be?" I answered that I would ask God for a map of my life, detailing every major event and decision. I wanted to see the big picture and know every turn in the road before I got there.

For some reason, God didn't provide that map. So I had to help Him. I sat down and mapped out my life: exactly where I would go, what I would do, and whom I would do it with. I knew which college I would attend and whom I would marry. Luckily, I met him when I was only sixteen. I had a chosen career—teacher, then mommy (but only two children). I found it calming to see my future so clearly. I knew exactly where I was going and what it would look like.

When I was in my early twenties, my life was still

going according to plan. I was old enough to have made several key decisions, but young enough to still believe I could manage my future without a lot of help from God. Everything was happening right on schedule.

Meet a nice man. Check.

Marry this nice man. Check.

Attend college and obtain my teaching credential. Check.

Next on my list: to have a baby or two.

It was time to check this item off my list.

I examined the calendar and chose a date that would be ideal for birthing a baby. Then I pulled out the charts, tracked my menstrual cycle, and chose my weekend for impregnation. Too much? What some might call *controlling*, others see as organized. My son Joel entered the world on schedule, in July 2001. I repeated this winning formula three years later, and in September 2004 we were rewarded with our beautiful daughter Hannah.

Family completed. Check.

But God ...

Don't you love those words? Or maybe they make your heart pound. Plenty of times I've been unsure about the *but God*s that suddenly interfered with my plans. But let me tell you, in the end He knows what He's doing.

There's not one single *but God* in my life that I look back on and count as a mistake. Oh, but some have been uncomfortable. Messy. Even painful. Yet God has only our best in mind. Always. "I know what I'm doing," God says. "I have it all planned out—plans to take care of you, not abandon you, plans to give you the future you hope for" (Jer. 29:11).

There've been times I was sailing smoothly along, taking care of things on my own—and then *bam!* A surprise *but God* appears. I am presented with a choice: Do I follow God's plan or mine? Do I say yes or no? He's promised to give the future I hope for. So do I take Him at His word? Do I trust His promise?

I'm strong-willed. Some might call me stubborn. I struggle with the whole submitting thing: to my husband or to God. The root of this issue is pride—in my own abilities to fix things, to know things, to figure things out. I like to think I'm right. I usually *am*. At least *sometimes*. But sometimes I'm wrong. I just don't always realize the difference until it's a little too late.

I was wrong about what my family would look like. I had it all planned, but life didn't go according to plan, at least according to *my* plan. It certainly went according to *His*. "We can make our plans, but the LORD determines our steps" (Prov. 16:9 NLT). I had made my plans, *but God* determined my steps. My plan for my family was good. *But God's* plan for my family was *great*.

I could have said no. I could have continued enjoying my good family. But I would never have experienced the *great* plans God had for me. I would never have been stretched, grown, and refined into who I am today. I would never have had the privilege of knowing four of my children. (I got a little teary-eyed writing that.) If I had turned my head, closed my eyes, and dug in my heels, I'd never have known the privilege of being a mother to six.

STORMS AND WHISPERS

Is there something in your life you might not even know is missing? Is there a tugging on your heart or a whisper in your ear you're working hard to ignore? It's easier to turn our heads and pretend we don't see where God is leading us. Instead, do the hard work of wrestling with it. Examine it. Poke holes in it. Question God. He can handle it.

I'm inspired by the Bible's account of when the prophet Elijah was surprised by some whispers from God. He was standing on a mountain, waiting to hear from God, because he had been told, "Go, stand on the mountain at attention before GOD. GOD will pass by" (1 Kings 19:11). Elijah obeyed. He stood at the top of that mountain. He was ready. And he thought he knew what he was ready for.

A hurricane wind ripped through the mountains and shattered the rocks before GOD, but GOD wasn't to be found in the wind; after the wind an earthquake, but GOD wasn't in the earthquake; and after the earthquake fire, but GOD wasn't in the fire; and after the fire a gentle and quiet whisper. (1 Kings 19:11–12)

In the past, God had shown up in some big ways. A pillar of fire. A column of smoke. A burning bush. Right before Elijah climbed the mountain, God had sent fire from heaven and burned up Baal's credibility. When Elijah stood on that mountain, he probably expected something big. Something that would rock his world and grab his attention. Something he couldn't ignore. Maybe a hurricane, an earthquake, or fire. *But God*, in His own time and in His own way, revealed His plans in a "gentle and quiet whisper."

What if Elijah had been so buffeted by the hurricane that he hadn't been listening? What if he'd still been shaking from the earthquake? What if he'd been burned out from the fire? His senses could easily have been so overwhelmed that he missed the whisper.

Today it's easy to get caught up in the storms of life. Yes, sometimes God strikes like a lightning bolt and awakens our senses. But sometimes God whispers. The only way we can hear His whisper is by listening closely.

When God whispered to the waiting Elijah, He said, "Go back the way you came" (1 Kings 19:15).

"Wait a minute," Elijah might have said. "What did You say? You were whispering, God. Maybe I didn't hear You. Did You say, 'Go back the way you came'? Why do You think I left in the first place? Don't You know that's not the easy way? There was danger back there! There was pain and struggle and dying."

Elijah had traveled forty miles through the desert to meet God on that mountaintop. Besides traveling toward God, he was also running from Queen Jezebel. Elijah had been living in her kingdom. Despite doing exactly what God told him, he faced death at the hands of the queen. So Elijah escaped and found God on the mountaintop to hear the new direction for his life.

But God did not give him a new direction. God told him to go back. Elijah was being led down a path that was sure to be filled with challenges.

DECISIONS

Elijah had a decision to make. So did I. Maybe you have a decision to make, too. Is God whispering something?

I heard a speaker share about the Hebrew phrase used for God's "gentle and quiet whisper." This phrase describes a very specific kind of whisper. The Hebrew words are *kol d'mama de kah*. It's the whispers a mother makes to her newborn after her child is first placed in her arms. They are whispers for her child's ears only, made when mother and infant are face-to-face, cheek-to-cheek.

Kol d'mama de kah is also used for the murmurings between two lovers in bed together. Those quiet sounds are barely audible because the two are pressed so close to each other.

And here, in 1 Kings 19, *kol d'mama de kah* is how God communicates with Elijah. The only reason Elijah could hear Him was because he was pressed so close to God. Elijah had climbed the mountain. He had drawn near to his Lord.

I think sometimes, even more than He wants us to hear His voice, God wants us to draw near to Him. He wants us to climb the mountain and press our faces to His and wait, expectantly.

I've found that every time God asks something, I have the choice to say yes or say no. Elijah said yes. Although the words were whispered, he heard God. Then he obeyed. He turned around and headed back into the *hard*, knowing he was never promised *easy*. Elijah obeyed because he knew that when he stood in the middle of the story God was writing for him, there would be joy. Even the hard becomes joy.

CHANGING PLANS

As I followed the map I had drawn for my life, I started to hear whispers from God. At first they were easy to ignore, since everything else in my life was so loud. Good things. God things. I've come to realize that if I'm not careful, good things can fill my schedule and my ears so loudly, I fail to hear God telling me about the next chapter He wants to write.

It began with my husband saying he felt God had something more for us. Scott often mentioned feeling stirred up, feeling we were on the verge of a new chapter in our lives. He was praying a new prayer for himself: *God, give me Your eyes. Help me to see what You see. Help me to love what You love. Break my heart for what breaks Yours.* This prayer was the spark that grew bigger and burned brighter until a new fire consumed our hearts. Scott didn't yet know to what we were being called, but he asked me to commit to pray about this with him.

I'm not a big fan of change. I like stability. I'm happiest when everyone follows *my* plan. My favorite things include:

- Lists with every item crossed off by the end of the day
- Advance notice for any changes to my schedule
- Husbands who complete their honey-do's in a timely manner

But my favorite things also include God. And prayer. And growth within myself. And within my husband. So I agreed to pray for God to do a new work in our hearts and our lives.

We prayed together in our bed before we went to sleep. We prayed individually in our quiet times and as we drove car pools. We prayed for open hearts, minds, and ears. We started sharing ideas and posing questions.

As I was cooking breakfast: "Is God asking us to move to a new city?"

While packing school lunches: "To become missionaries?"

At the family dinner table: "To support a new ministry? To volunteer?"

Brushing our teeth side by side in the master bathroom: "To start a new business?"

Waking up as the sun broke the horizon: "To adopt?"

Wait a minute.

Adopt? Where did that idea come from? We had agreed years ago that we would never adopt. Before we said our marriage vows, we promised each other that adoption would never be a part of our story. We both had been burned when we'd gotten too close to adoption and foster care. Yet here he stood, barefoot in the walk-in closet, dropping heavy words before I'd even had my first cup of coffee.

It felt important, that moment in the closet. As

Scott's words filled the space between us, I felt a stutter step in my heart. Not a good, warm heart-quickening. More like a flutter of panic. It felt like those might be God's whispered words. I wasn't sure I wanted to hear them.

In the months that followed, amid our discussions, research, questions, and prayer, God whispered again and again to my heart, *Yes. This.*

He whispered it through the lives of our friends. Chris and Jessica had adopted four children and birthed three others. They made life in a large family look fun, attractive, and joyful. If they could do it, maybe we could too. As we sat across the coffee table from our friends and asked our questions and listed our concerns, they assured us we could.

God whispered it through the death of my husband's best friend. As Peter battled cancer in the hope that he could spend more time with his children here on earth, he also prepared his soul to spend eternity with his Father in heaven. Staring death in the face has a way of bringing one's life into focus. What is most important? As we sat next to Peter's bed with his wife, children, and parents as his breathing shuddered to a stop, we were reminded that our lives are but a vehicle for God's plan.

Late one night when my house was sleeping, I sat in bed and read again the verse I had been reading during these months: "Pure and undefiled religion in the sight of our God and Father is this: to visit orphans and widows in their distress, and to keep oneself unstained by the world" (James 1:27 NASB). I had convinced myself I was searching for God's will. But in reality I was searching those words for a hidden escape hatch.

Then I prayed, *Make it clear, God. You know me. I want a road map. Can You please show me where I should turn? Shall I continue in my life, going straight ahead? Or is this the fork in the road? God, is this what You have for me? For our family? Do You want us to adopt?*

Right there in my bed, with my feet tucked under the blanket and my Bible on my knees, I felt God say, *Natalie, why would I say no? I already answered you in that book you are holding. Who do you think wrote those words? Care for the orphans. If you are willing to adopt, why would I say no?*

At that moment, I gave in to God. I acknowledged that I heard His whispers. I agreed to follow Him down this new path on our family's map. I said yes.

As soon as we made that decision and stepped into this uncharted area, road signs began to appear. We walked forward, and God provided the directional arrows. Our job was to learn to read them.

5

SUBMITTED VESSELS

The following is an excerpt from a conversation that took place at my kitchen table during the first home visit from our social worker:

SW: How many children would you be interested in adopting?

Scott: I can see us adopting up to four children.

Me: *What?* No. He means one or two children. He leaves and goes to work every day. I stay home. I need to be honest about how many children I can handle.

SW: What age range of children would you be willing to adopt?

Scott: Anything up to age ten.

Me: *What?* No. We want to maintain birth order in this home. Let's go with anything up to age five. That seems much more manageable.

SW: What about special needs? Medical conditions? Are you open to any children with
   special circumstances?

Scott: Yes.

Me: *What?* No. He meant to say no to that question. Obviously.

SW: Where are you thinking about adopting?
   Domestically? Internationally? Which country?

Scott: Ethiopia. I think God is saying Ethiopia.

Me: Yes. He finally got an answer right. Ethiopia.

When we said yes to God and stepped into the next
chapter in our story, we had no idea what we were
doing. Actually, we still don't. But we're getting better at relying on God's expertise instead of our own.

We'd never seen inside the world of adoption. All
the terminology, the never-ending paperwork, and
the hoops we had to jump through were all new to
us. It wasn't as easy as we thought to open up our
home and add to our family through adoption. There
were a million decisions to be made, and we hadn't
yet made any of them. The only thing we knew for
sure was that we both felt tugged toward Ethiopia.

I think the reason for this was that Ethiopia was
where our children lived. We didn't know it yet, but
God did. Our children were living in Ethiopia.

Yes, plenty of children in America need some
loving. In 2013 there were more than 400,000 children in the nation's foster care system. That means

400,000 hearts who needed some tender, loving care; 400,000 little bodies who needed a bed to sleep in; and 400,000 souls who longed for a home. There's a desperate need for families willing to help.

There are also plenty of orphans in countries around the world who are waiting and alone. Worldwide, some 140 million children have lost one or both parents. This number does not include children who are living on the streets, are exploited or trafficked, or who have been forced into military groups. If 140 million orphans sounds overwhelming, that's because it is. There's simply no way to help all the world's hurting children.

But there's a way to help one. Or two. Or four.

How did we look at those numbers, see the great need, and choose where and how and whom? We followed God's instructions.

If I really believe God has a better plan for my life, knows the beginning from the end, knit me together in my mother's womb, and knows the number of hairs on my head—then I also believe God knows my children. God is the Master Builder. He is building my family. I simply have to follow His instructions.

You know me inside and out, you know every bone in my body; you know exactly how I was made, bit by bit, how I was sculpted from nothing into something. Like an open book, you watched me grow from conception to birth; all the stages of my life were spread out before you, the days of my life all prepared before I'd even lived one day. (Psalm 139:15–16)

Did you hear that? "All the stages of my life were spread out before you, the days of my life all prepared before I'd even lived one day." God says it. I truly believe it. The rub lies in living it day to day. Back when I was in college, I had asked God to reach down and spread open wide the map of my life so I could see what He sees.

He didn't do that. After all, if I had the instructions spread out in front of me, I wouldn't need to be in constant communication with the Master Builder. And oh, He desires a relationship with me. With me! And you. We are—each and every one of us—His beloveds.

While He was busy building our family, He was also building our relationship. His and mine. Because of this journey, our relationship has grown closer and stronger. It has been refined by the fire of adoption.

As my husband and I sat at our kitchen table with the social worker, drinking coffee and answering questions, we realized how much we didn't know:

- Which adoption agency?
- Domestic or international?
- What is our timeline?

- How much will this cost?
- Whom, how many, and how old?

We had no idea. We knew nothing.

Over the next year, as we completed our background checks and our fingerprinting, our paperwork and our family dossier, as we sent checks for money we didn't have and trusted God to provide for what He had called us to do, God whispered again and again to my heart: *Kol d'mama de ka.* Softly and gently, He whispered.

His first whisper sounded much like my husband's voice, there at the kitchen table as our social worker asked her questions. But my stubbornness is no great secret. I wasn't ready to listen the first time. To get my attention, God had to speak a little louder and more often.

Sometimes His whispers came through conversations. I contacted a friend who was not only a social worker, but also an adoptive mother. She was willing to answer all my questions. She told me her story. I told her mine. We wondered what story my future children might have to tell.

Abby talked about the orphan crisis in Ethiopia. The details she provided left me overwhelmed. She talked of the poorly staffed government orphanages with a shortage of food and medicine and never enough diapers or caregivers. She said children are stacked in rows in their cribs, lying in their own filth. I sat in Abby's tastefully decorated living room and cried.

Sometimes I heard God's whispers when reading at night before bed. Besides reading through the Bible, I worked my way through *The Connected Child* and *Adopted for Life*.

In *There Is No Me Without You* by Melissa Fay Greene, I read about the plight of orphans in Ethiopia who test positive for HIV. They are the un-wanted, the forgotten, the shunned. The medication that could save their lives is cheap and readily avail-able. But it has to be given on a strict schedule. It has to be given with food. Both of those things, a schedule and food, are impossible without someone around who cares. So these children are dying, not from a lack of medication, but from a lack of love.

As I crunched numbers and looked at expenses, I heard God promise to provide. I wouldn't say I was worried, but I wondered how we would pay for everything.

After dinner with our friends Chris and Jessica, we walked them and their seven children to their car. Under the pale moonlight, at first I didn't see the check they handed to us. A check they'd subtracted from their own budget to add to ours. Unsolicited, at just the right time to encourage, we received our first adoption donation—$1,000.

Sometimes God whispered in my ear when I ̶ ̶ ̶ washing the dishes or folding the laundry. I l

Him whisper we should adopt more than one child: *How about a sibling set?*

Okay, God. Sibling set means two. I will adopt two children.

What about those big sibling sets? The ones that are hard to find families for? What about a sibling set of four?

What, God? You were whispering. I think You said three. Okay. I will agree to a sibling set of three.

I heard Him when He whispered that we should adopt older children: *How about older than five?*

Okay, God. One of my siblings can be older than five. But the others should be little. Toddlers and babies are preferable.

Let's wait and see about that, God seemed to say. *Maybe I will give you older children.*

I am pretty sure I can help You find a sibling set with at least one baby.

I heard Him when He whispered that we should be open to adopting special-needs children or those with medical conditions. *What about an HIV-positive child? Would you consider loving and caring for one of My children who is sick?*

The final recommendation from our social worker looked like this: "The family is approved for up to four children, ages zero to ten, including HIV-positive and other medical needs."

It sounded pretty close to the description Scott had given a year earlier at the beginning of our process. It would have been a lot easier if I had just listened the first time God whispered to me. But my heart needed time to get on board. God allowed me that time.

Now I had to follow His example and also learn to be patient. Because as soon as we finished our paperwork and sent it off to Ethiopia, we began the wait to see our children's faces for the first time. And if there's one thing I am (besides being a planner and stubborn), it's impatient.

Don't I sound like a perfect mother? I'll let you in on a little secret: I'm not. I am not a perfect mother. But I proudly claim the title of World's Okayest Mom, and that's good enough for me. I've learned God is not looking for a perfect vessel to carry out His work. We all are broken vessels. We all are clay pots. "We carry this precious Message around in the unadorned clay pots of our ordinary lives" (2 Cor. 4:7).

I recognize myself in those words. I am living an ordinary life. It is God who provides the extraordinary.

There is an old Sunday school song that goes like this:

You don't have to be strong
You don't have to have money
You don't have to be smart
You don't have to be funny
You don't have to be the biggest
You don't have to be the best

You just have to be willing
You just have to say YES.

God is not looking for a perfect vessel, He is looking for a submitted vessel. God writes the very best stories through His submitted vessels. We just have to be willing. We just have to say yes.

6

OKAYEST MOM

When you first saw this book, you might have had the wrong idea about me. Maybe you thought I excelled at laundry and parented with the perfect balance of love and logic. Let me set you straight. The parenting thing is a little iffy. I do, however, really know my way around a laundry room. Laundry is my area of expertise. Parenting isn't. Writing this book doesn't make me an expert.

I'm constantly learning just how much I don't know. I make a lot of mistakes. I often laugh at myself. I often have to ask for forgiveness.

But boy do I try hard. I dig in. I ask for help. I lean on God. I do the best I can day by day, and I know God will fill in the rest.

I trust that God does not require any more of me than that. He knows I'm a clay pot. He designed me that way.

As I see all the other moms, I realize every one of us is walking around with broken edges. In one way or another, we all are cracked. At best, we can aspire to become okayest moms, and that's just the way it's going to be—not perfect moms. Sometimes we can get caught in the trap of trying to project a better image to the public. We try to hide the cracks and cover up the ordinary. We use photo editing and filters to adorn our plain, cracked clay pots.

In this world of selfies and sound bites, we have the opportunity to mold our public images into pretty much anything we want. I do it too. By nature I tend to be an oversharer, but there are some things I keep to myself because I don't want others to think less of me.

But the truth is, I *am* less! Not in a bad way. But in a real way. I just can't do it all—or be it all or say it all in just the right way. And that's okay! Less of me, Jesus, and more of You!

It's time for us okayest moms to be honest with one another. We all are okay. Some days are great. Some days are not. Some days we have enough patience and love to last from sunrise to sunset, and we even have a "little something" left over for our husbands at the end of the day. But some days our kids eat Pop-Tarts in their pajamas at noon amid the piles of dirty laundry, and when our husbands look at us with googly eyes we are like, "If *one more* person wants to touch me today, I will *hurt* them."

We usually want to share about only those first kinds of days and keep quiet about the second. But we *all* have those kinds of days!

In a spirit of camaraderie, and to help you better understand my special brand of crazy, I now share with you my very own Top Five okayest mom moments:

1. **I once forgot to put the peanut butter in my son's peanut butter and jelly sandwich. I also forgot the jelly.**

   When I picked up my kids from school, the first thing Micah said was "Mom, why did you send empty bread to school for my lunch?"

   "Empty bread? Whatever do you mean?"

   "At lunch when I tried to eat my sandwich, all I tasted was bread. There was no peanut butter or jelly."

   "Oh, honey. You must be mistaken. Maybe I didn't spread the peanut butter and jelly all the way to the edges. You just needed to eat into the center of the sandwich a little bit more."

   "That's what I thought, too, so I took a bite out of the middle, but there was nothing there! Look, Mom!" He held up his "sandwich," which had a big, round bite missing from the middle.

   Not only did I send my son to school with only bread for his lunch, I also tried to shift the responsibility for the mistake off my shoulders and onto his. Way to go, World's Okayest Mom.

2. **Once I wrote this note to my child's teacher:**

No. I cannot make several loaves of homemade bread to send to class on Friday. I never make homemade bread. I don't believe I have ever made homemade bread, even once in my life, and I am certainly not going to start now. It sounds like too much work. Please ask some other mom to do this. Preferably a mom with fewer children. In place of homemade bread, I volunteer to bring a bag of candy. [I may be paraphrasing, but only slightly.]

Thankfully, my husband intercepted my note. He saw it on top of my child's folder and said, "Honey! Why would you write a note like this?"

And I said, "Because I have six children, and this teacher has no children—and obviously no idea of the amount of energy that six children can suck out of you. I'm tired, and I don't believe in homemade bread."

Cooler heads prevailed and I did not send the note. I also did not make homemade bread. I went to a bakery, bought several loaves of "homemade" bread, and delivered them to the classroom. And when I walked into the classroom, there was another mom demonstrating how to make homemade bread. She talked about how she buys her flour from a local flour mill and bakes bread for her family—every week. And she has *eight* children. Too bad I have only six. That's my excuse for not baking.

3. **I lied—in front of my kids. And they caught me.**

You know that perfect mom? The one who looks good and smells good and dresses good and *is* so good inside that her heart just shines out of her do-gooder, perfectly made-up eyes that have almost no wrinkles around them. She's probably a World's Okayest Mom, too, just like the rest of us.

One time a perfect mom planned a party. She made up adorable, color-coordinated invitations. They even came with a preparty activity for my child to complete and take to the festivity. This mom sent home the invitation with my child from school. And she asked for an RSVP.

I forgot to RSVP.

One day, as all my children were loading into the minivan at school, and backpacks and elbows were flying everywhere, and I was slightly distracted by the dog who had just peed on the upholstery, and I had not showered that day, I heard a tap on my window.

I turned to see this mom standing there with a kind and beautiful smile.

I slowly rolled down the window.

She asked if I had gotten the invitation and if my child would be attending the party.

Why didn't I just say I had forgotten? I don't know what came over me, but out came the words "What invitation? I don't think I saw any invitation."

From the backseat my child said, "Yes, you did, Mom. I gave it to you last week."

Why did I lie? I have no idea. I'd like to blame fumes from what the dog had just done. Maybe they addled my brain.

I have since repented and asked for forgiveness from my children and from God. Maybe someday I'll get around to apologizing to this other mom. I hope she's not reading this book right now.

4. **I forgot one of my children.**

Seriously. After I buckled up my other five children, I drove away and left one child at home. You know what it's like.

We were trying to get to church on time. I was hurrying everyone along.

"Come on, children! We don't want to be late! Get your shoes on and put that lizard back outside and stop pinching your brother's arm and yes, honey, your hair looks delightful and *get in the car right now* because *we cannot be late to worship the Lord God Almighty!*"

Whew! I did it. We were all (or so I thought) in the car and headed to church. Then my oldest son said from the backseat, "Hey, Mom. Where's Leah?"

Yep. I forgot a child. She had been in her room with the door closed and had somehow missed my gentle proddings to get everyone out the door.

Fortunately, she was still in her room with the door closed when we came back for her, blissfully unaware that anything unusual had happened.

5. **I forgot my friend's children.**

This is worse than #4 because this time, I forgot *four* children. And this time the children were aware of the mishap.

My dear friend Jessica had asked a favor of me. An easy thing, really. Our children attend the same school. After school Jessica and I were meeting at the gym. Would I mind picking up her four children and meeting her there?

Sure. No problem. Anything for a friend.

So I went to the school, drove through the pickup line, loaded up my children, waved at her children, and drove to the gym.

As I was about to get my sweats on, my phone rang. It was Jessica. Whatever could she want?

The school had just called her to ask where

she was. It seems no one had shown up that day to gather her children. Her little darlings were in after-school care until someone could come and pick them up.

I felt so bad, I cried! But Jessica is a true friend, and she assured me it wasn't a big deal. She forgave me.

On a completely unrelated note, Jessica has never again asked me to pick up her children. (So if you'd like to be excused from the carpool rotation, you could borrow this idea.)

Here's the thing. We *all* have moments like this. Yes, some of them are worse than others, but not one of us is perfect. We aren't meant to be. If we were perfect, why would we need a savior? If we could do it all on our own, we wouldn't need to rely on God.

We may not be perfect, but we are the perfect mamas for our children.

We are enough.

We are daughters of the King. And *He* is perfect!

Somewhere along the way, between the lying and the dog urine and the forgotten children, I have learned some things. Certainly not everything. But some things. And so have all of us—even the most flustered. I bet we all know more—and do more and love more—than we give ourselves credit for. We're hard on ourselves. And we can be hard on one another. We look in the mirror and glance right past the beauty to focus on the wrinkles, the gray hair, and the imperfections.

Okay, we have wrinkles. Mine get deeper every day. I like to call them smile lines. If those smile lines are any indication, I'm a very happy person.

Yes, we have gray hair. If you have a really good stylist and lots of money to cover it up, though, go for it. "Gray hair is a mark of distinction, the award for a God-loyal life" (Prov. 16:31).

Yes, we are beautiful—wrinkles, gray hair, and all.

Yes, we make mistakes. But we also do things right. Both, ladies. It's both.

We are the World's Okayest Moms.

7

PERMANENT

The first and only time I permed my hair I was eleven. We were in no position to afford a professional hairstylist, so a home permanent sounded like a good alternative. My mother pulled out those long, pink wormlike rods and skimmed the instructions. Then she discarded the instructions and went with her gut. I trusted her.

I am not laying the blame solely on her. We both were at fault. She separated my hair into sections, wrapped each section around a pink rod, applied the chemicals, and settled a plastic shower cap over my head. The instructions recommended wearing this getup for thirty minutes.

By the fifteen-minute mark, my scalp was burning. This might have been because of the damage done by previous treatments for lice. Or it might have been because my mother had applied every last drop of the permanent solution, whether I needed it or not.

But it wasn't only the burning sensation, which I overplayed just a bit. I was impatient to see my new, glorious curls. I convinced my mother that fifteen minutes was plenty of time for the perm to set, so we should move on to the next step. At this point my mother wasn't following the instructions anyway, so what was an extra fifteen minutes?

It turns out those extra minutes were important. The finished product was a head full of half-baked curls, frizzy and pointing at various angles, plus several sections of straight hair that had failed to retain any curl. I was certainly glorious, or something close to it.

With a drama reserved for preteen girls, I wailed, cried, and fretted myself to school the next morning. Sadly, things went no better than I had feared. Kids can be cruel.

We ended up cutting off most of my hair. There was no other way to fix it.

The good news is that one year later, I hit puberty. The hormones that began coursing through my body also managed to curl my hair! From birth to age twelve—with the exception of the days surrounding my home permanent—I had straight hair. But from puberty on—glorious curls!

There are two points to this story.

Point one. You should hire a professional for any of

your perming needs. Failing this, you should at least follow the instructions.

Point two. Patience has never been my virtue. Whether waiting for my hair to curl when I was eleven or waiting for God to complete our family when I was thirty-five, my impatience usually got the best of me. I think this is one of the reasons God gave me my husband at such a young age.

We began our adoption journey by praying, "God, give us Your eyes. Help us to see what You see. Break our hearts for what breaks Yours." We sincerely wanted to do whatever God asked. We wanted to obey Him and follow wherever He might lead. Along the way, the desire to follow God's heart also changed our own hearts. During those days, weeks, and months, as we prepared our home and our paperwork, we were also creating space in our lives and our hearts for our new children. We started to fall in love with them.

We saw their faces in our friend's referral photos. We read their stories in the online support groups for adoptive parents. We heard their voices in the countless videos our agency shared. While we didn't yet know the specifics, every heartbreaking story became our children's heartache. Every tear was one more tear we were not there to wipe away.

A year had passed by the time our dossier was completed and sent to Ethiopia. A year! That should have been plenty of time for God to set things in place. We had listened to His voice and followed His leading. We had done all that He asked. Now it was His turn. We could do nothing but wait.

We completed the application in July 2011. Then I sat down and prepared myself for the call that would tell us who our children were. The call was sure to come any day.

Only it didn't.

It didn't come the next morning, the morning after that, the next week, or the next month. *What is the holdup, God?* I was pretty sure He was running late on His building-a-family promise. I filled my days with rearranging bedrooms, buying and washing new sheets and comforters, painting and decorating, and preparing for the children who would surely be coming home soon.

I walked the aisles of Target and picked out pajamas for the little bodies that would need to be kept warm at night. I went to the bookstore and found new bedtime stories to whisper into little ears. I carefully chose a special stuffed animal that would be cuddled until the stuffing leaked out. At Christmas I bought presents for all of my children: the children I already held in my arms and the children I held only in my heart. I basically drove myself crazy.

Then we turned the calendar to a new year. We entered 2012 with no children sleeping in those empty bedrooms. In the adoption world, it's common for families to wait months or even years after they complete their paperwork. But many of those families were waiting to adopt babies or toddlers. Many were adopting only one or two children—healthy children with no known medical conditions. Our situation was different. Because we were so flexible, we were in a much shorter line. A line we expected to move quickly.

Every night as I tucked Joel and Hannah into bed, I prayed with them, kissed their cheeks, and wondered what my children were doing on the other side of the world. I didn't understand the delay. If there were so many children needing a family, and we were a family needing our children, why should we be stalled by bureaucrats and paperwork?

During this time of waiting, I found a lullaby:

Kisses in the Wind
(The Waiting Child's Lullaby)

I hold you in my heart and touch you in my dreams.

You are here each day with me, at least that's how it seems.

I know you wonder where we are ... what's taking us so long.

But remember, child, I love you so and God will keep you strong.

Now go outside and feel the breeze and let it touch your skin ...

Because tonight, just as always, I blow you kisses
in the wind.

May God hold you in His hand until I can be
with you.
I promise you, my darling, I'm doing all that I
can do.
Very soon, you'll have a family for real, not just
pretend.
But for tonight, just as always, I blow you kisses
in the wind.
May God wrap you in His arms and hold you
very tight.
And let the angels bring the kisses that I send to
you each night.
—Pamela Durkota, written for Josh

I was such a basket case. It's never taken much to
make me cry: a Hallmark movie, a Cheerios com-
mercial, a perfect cup of coffee. Still, I would read
these words full of big emotions almost every night.

Ethiopia's time zone is ten hours ahead of California. I knew my children were living their lives
before me. I could never quite catch up to those
hours, minutes, and moments I was missing. When
my sun was setting, theirs was rising. When I sat
down to dinner, I wondered what they were having
for breakfast. Did they even have anything to eat for
breakfast?

I knew all the statistics of my children's homeland. Ethiopia is home to more than 4.3 million orphans. One in six children will die before their fifth birthday. There is only one doctor for every 24,000 people in Ethiopia. More than 80 percent of the population survive on less than $1 a day. The numbers are enough to make the most stoic person weep. I am not stoic.

Waiting for an adoption referral is like being pregnant *forever*. It's having all the hormones and emotions and weight gain—caused by a combination of stress and overeating—but no firm due date. You might give birth today or two years from now. No one knows! So hurry up and wait, Mama. Instead of your child being safely cocooned inside your body, he or she is half a world away, living in conditions you know are less than ideal.

No wonder I started to feel a little anxious, unnerved, and slightly unhinged. What to do to calm my frazzled nerves?

I got a tattoo.

I needed some evidence that my children and I were connected—that they existed in more than my dreams. A tattoo seemed the sanest solution.

I walked into a tattoo parlor with a drawing of the word for "family" in the language my children could understand. The Amharic word is *betasub*. When I left that tattoo parlor an hour later, my new family was a permanent part of me.

Besides tattooing my wrist, I pursued other beneficial activities to calm my anxious heart. I read, prayed, and found an online Bible study. I realized more and more that *waiting* and *hoping* are wound together like two strands of the same rope. Waiting involves anticipation and expectation—a confident hope in something that will take place. The ability to wait on the Lord stems from being confident and focused on who God is and what He is doing.

Waiting is not a passive activity. We are not merely existing; we are actively involved. We are expectant. We anticipate God's movement in our lives. In 1 Kings 19, when Elijah hears God's voice, Elijah isn't going about his daily life. He isn't lying around doing nothing. He isn't hiding in the cave. Yes, he had been doing those things. Then God got ahold of him.

[Elijah] fell asleep under the lone broom bush. Suddenly an angel shook him awake and said, "Get up and eat!" He looked around and, to his surprise, right by his head were a loaf of bread baked on some coals and a jug of water. He ate the meal and went back to sleep. The angel of GOD came back, shook him awake again, and said, "Get up and eat some more—you've got a long journey ahead of you." He got up, ate and drank his fill, and set out. Nourished by that meal, he walked forty days and nights, all the way to the mountain of God, to Horeb. When he got there, he crawled into a cave and went to sleep. Then the word of GOD

came to him: "So Elijah, what are you doing here?"
"I've been working my heart out for the GOD-of-the-
Angel-Armies," said Elijah. "The people of Israel have
abandoned your covenant, destroyed the places of wor-
ship, and murdered your prophets. I'm the only one left,
and now they're trying to kill me." Then he was told,
"Go, stand on the mountain at attention before GOD.
GOD will pass by." (1 Kings 19:5–11)

Elijah was done with sleeping under bushes and lying about in caves. He was done with simply existing. He became an active participant. He walked forty days and nights. He climbed the mountain and stood at the top, ready for whatever might come his way. He was hopeful. He was confident. He was waiting on the Lord.

I, too, was waiting on the Lord to build my family. I was learning to place my confidence in God's abilities rather than my own.

Please don't skip over the next part. (I know I tend to skim or jump ahead when an author throws in some Bible verses to make a point.) Stick with me. Read these next three passages from Isaiah 40. Feel them. They inspire confidence and hope, an expectation that God is moving.

Who has scooped up the ocean in his two hands,
or measured the sky between his thumb and little
finger . . . ? (v. 12)

God sits high above the round ball of earth. The people look like mere ants. He stretches out the skies like a canvas—yes, like a tent canvas to live under. He ignores what all the princes say and do. The rulers of the earth count for nothing. (vv. 22–23)

Why would you ever complain, O Jacob, or whine, Israel, saying, "GOD has lost track of me. He doesn't care what happens to me"? Don't you know anything? Haven't you been listening? GOD doesn't come and go. God lasts. He's Creator of all you can see or imagine. He doesn't get tired out, doesn't pause to catch his breath. And he knows everything, inside and out. (vv. 27–28)

That is good stuff, solid and meaty. You can sink your teeth into it and hold on. If God knows us inside and out—if He ignores what the princes say and do, and the rulers of the earth count for nothing—then He knows exactly what's happening in Ethiopia. He must have a reason for the months that passed by while my children lived on the other side of the world from me.

We turned the calendar page to February without receiving a call. Although my head agreed with the concept of waiting expectantly on God, this hadn't yet taken hold in my heart.

Knowing something and living it out are often two very different enterprises. I decided God might need a little help, so I started searching databases of waiting children.

There are many online lists of children who need families. Some of these children are sick and need families willing to take on their special medical needs. Some are above age three, considered old in the adoption world. Some are sibling sets looking for families willing to adopt many children at once.

I scrolled through pictures and profiles and wondered if this one, that one, or maybe these children right in front of me were my children. As I clicked on story after painful story, I searched for our children's faces.

Then I found them. I saw a picture, read a profile, and thought, *These children. Maybe these are my children.* It was a sibling set of three, all of them HIV-positive and one of them only a baby, waiting in an orphanage in Ethiopia.

I printed out their picture and brought it to the dinner table that night. I showed my husband and read him the details of their life story. "What do you think, honey?" I asked him. "Maybe this is our family." I saw their picture for the first time on Monday, February 20, 2012.

On Tuesday, February 21, I sent away for their file. I received their medical records and family history, and I pored over the documents. I faxed copies of their blood work and doctor's notes to my pediatrician. I called the local HIV clinic and asked questions. I cleared my schedule for the rest of that day. I thought of nothing else.

On Wednesday my husband and I needed to make a decision. We had completed all of our paperwork with the adoption agency we had been working with for the past year. But the children whose file I held were not represented by our agency. To pursue these children, we would have to switch. Not an insurmountable obstacle, but it would mean losing a big chunk of our deposit and repaying that money to the new agency.

Wednesday night Scott and I filled out the paperwork for this new agency. We wrote a check and clipped it all together in a stack on our countertop. The next morning we would send those papers and the money to the other agency. We would pursue this new avenue.

Then we climbed into bed and held hands. Scott prayed and asked for clarity. He asked for wisdom. He prayed that God would guide our steps and that we would follow Him wherever He led us. Scott has always been eloquent in his prayers.

I've always been a straightforward prayer. I prayed only one thing: "God, if this is not the door we are meant to walk through, You need to close it. Otherwise, tomorrow morning I am walking through this door."

So many other people might have been better at this. Better at listening to God. Better at waiting.

Better at mothering. I'm talking about those calm, spiritual, gentle souls who are very good at not letting their desires lead the way. I tend to adopt a headstrong approach. As in, "God, stop me if You don't want me to do this. Because I am already moving forward and getting things done."

But God did not choose any of those other people for this task. He chose me. Knowing all of my weaknesses, He chose me. Which once again proves we don't need to be perfect. We simply need to be willing to obey God.

> *We can make our plans, but the LORD determines our steps. (Proverbs 16:9 NLT)*

I know I've already discussed this verse. But I needed to be reminded of it again and again. It's almost as though God wrote this verse specifically for me. I can make my plans—or write my lists or fill out paperwork to switch adoption agencies—as much as I want, but He will determine where I actually end up.

On Thursday, February 23, Scott took the pile of paper and the check with him to work. He was going to send it out with the day's mail. Soon afterward I rolled through the drop-off line at school, kissed my children good-bye, and drove to the gym. As I stood in the group fitness room, my phone rang. Scott was calling to tell me to come to his office.

Our current agency was trying to reach us. They had requested a phone call for 11:00 a.m., and they asked that both of us be present.

I forgot about my workout and drove to my husband's office. Something big was happening. I could feel it. Our agency had never scheduled a phone call like this.

My husband and I sat behind his desk with our chairs pulled close. I looked out the window at the river that runs behind his office, the sunlight reflecting off the water and blinding me with its brightness. Our hands were joined, and I felt Scott's sticky palm against mine. A voice came over the speakerphone and filled the office.

And I knew. Before anything of substance was said, I knew. This was God showing up, right now. He was answering my prayer. He was closing *my* door and opening *His*.

8

SHUKRIYA'S PRAYERS

Ethiopia, 2012

Shukriya lay in her bed and squeezed her hands so tightly, her fingers ached. "God," she whispered into the dark void, "please let me see my sister again."

She tried to block the sounds of the other children rustling in the night, but there was no hope for quiet when you lived in an orphanage. The girl in the bunk below hummed softly. Shukriya's single blanket, pulled tight around her body, gave scant protection against the fears that invaded her dreams.

"God, I know You can hear me. I know You are here with me. Please bring my sister back."

She prayed the same prayer every night, long after the lights were turned off and the orphans were left to lie alone in their beds. She prayed long after the other children drifted to sleep. Long after there seemed any hope of an answer.

Shukriya lay in the dark and remembered the last time she had seen her sister. Despite the harsh Ethiopian sun, fear had chilled her heart as she watched her sister being led away. Those people—those strangers—had promised they would take care of Hamdiya. But Shukriya had not liked the way they looked at her, as though she were no better than one of the stray dogs that wandered the barren fields. She had not liked the way they grabbed Hamdiya's arm and hurried her down the road, away from her family.

Shukriya had watched her sister's back get smaller and smaller, straining her eyes until everything blurred. Then she had turned and walked home, shoulders sagging, chest tight with unshed tears. She would not cry. She would not make her mother feel any worse than she already did.

Everything in Shukriya's life had changed that day. Shortly after saying good-bye to their sister, Shukriya and her little brothers had also said good-bye to their mother. She had brought them to this orphanage. She hugged them and kissed them, then walked away and left them behind.

For two years they had lived in the orphanage. Two years of monotony. Every day was the same. And every night, Shukriya lay in bed and talked to God. She poured out all of her fears. She knew He was listening.

"Please, God. Find a new family for me. And please find my sister. I want to see her again." She cried as she fell asleep.

The next morning dawned bright and hot. The orphanage looked the same as it always did by daylight: dirty, barren, and lonely. Shukriya's heart felt much the same while she stood in line at the rain barrel. She used the dirty water to wash her face and rinse her feet. Running her hand over her bald head, she remembered her thickly tangled curls. They were gone, along with everything else from her old life. Because of the lice that thrived amid the unsanitary conditions, the nannies had shaved her head.

She washed her hands as well as she could, then walked to pick up her breakfast bowl. She missed the fresh vegetables they had grown on her family's farm, but at least the rice filled her stomach.

The only bright spot in Shukriya's day were the hours she got to see her little brothers. They were allowed to spend their afternoons together, there in the dirt courtyard.

Shukriya invented games to keep them entertained. She found an old piece of string and tied it into a loop. Winding it through their fingers, she made up elaborate rules for twisting and turning and pulling it into shapes. She took turns giving them piggyback rides, one after the other, until her back ached low and dull, the way it had after she'd carried water jugs on her head for many hours. She found a rock and used it as a marker for a jumping game, letting her brothers win time and again.

And always she prayed. Constantly. Continuously. She wasn't sure whom she was talking to, but she knew there must be a God who was listening. She felt Him nearby, especially in the night. When she was most afraid, she could feel Him wrap His arms around her. It felt like being hugged by her father. She hoped one day she might have another father who would hold her close.

Until that day came, *if* that day ever came, she was determined to keep holding on to the hope of something better. The hope of a brighter tomorrow.

9

HE CALLS US BY NAME

When I was eight and a half months pregnant with my first child, I heaved myself out of bed early one morning to use the bathroom. As I waddled across the tile floor, my water broke. My darling husband, who did the cleanup, was grateful it didn't happen until I was off the carpet.

Likewise, it was a good thing we rushed ourselves straight to the hospital, because a mere twenty-six agonizing hours later, my firstborn son entered the world.

I believe in anesthesia, epidurals, and caffeine. I needed all three to birth and raise my babies. So I believe some sort of God-given amnesia must be at work when women decide to have a second baby, or another after that. We forget the torturous hours of labor, the hot-knife pain that cuts through our stomachs, the tearing and ripping of important body parts that, despite thirteen stitches, will never be quite the same again. We endure the sleepless nights and the colicky crying, the stretch marks and the sciatica. Then we decide to do it again.

Adoption is a little different, but not much. The pain, the tearing, and the stretch marks might not be as apparent to a casual observer, but they are very real. The scars are not physical; they are emotional. And heaven help me, they might be worse.

As we sat in my husband's office that February day, with the now-discarded pile of paperwork that represented my own plans sitting beside the phone, we had no idea of the joy and the struggle that lay in store. I look back at that naive optimism and I see it as a gift. A sort of "pre-amnesia" that allowed us to rush headlong into the pain. On that day our lives were forever changed, our future spread out before us like some glittering treasure map.

We failed to see the sticky mire, the deep pits, and the crumbled ruins that marked the road before us. We thought we were prepared. We had read all the books, taken all the classes, and asked all the questions. But as we heard our social worker's voice over the speakerphone, we could not have begun to imagine the journey on which God was about to take us.

In that moment, all of my waiting and hoping threaded together. As I heard the words for which I'd been waiting, those strands in the rope that tied my future and my past were pulled taut. On the same

Thursday morning I had told God I was going to walk through a new door that led to my own plans, He firmly closed that door and directed us down His path for our family. That path led to the children He had chosen for us. On that sunny day in February, we heard our children's names for the first time:

- Shukriya, age seven, a quiet girl who plays peacemaker among her friends in the orphanage
- Eba, age six, a jokester who is constantly pulling pranks and searching for laughter
- Eyob, age four, everyone's darling; always on the move, always talking, always mischievous

Siblings. Three of them. A girl and two boys. My children.

We opened the email and clicked on the pictures. For the first time we looked into their eyes. Our children gazed at us from the computer screen, their dark eyes full of uncertainty, so closely mirroring our own feelings as we looked into an unknown future together.

We saw Eba's gap-toothed grin and too-thin arms. We saw Shukriya's shy smile and her intense desire to please. We saw Eyob's fierce determination, masking the fear he hid deep inside.

Tears fell as we read their history and learned about the circumstances that had brought them to this point: Surviving in an orphanage in Ethiopia.

Waiting and dreaming of the day a new family might come for them.

We sat side by side in my husband's office, our children's names hanging in the air between us, and God began to reframe our idea of what our family looked like. As the sun's rays danced across our children's faces on the computer screen, we felt our hearts expand. We suddenly found more space inside. Space that was waiting to be filled with the pieces our family had been missing all along.

We began the long process of getting to know these precious souls. Of beginning to love these three specific children God had given to us. From that first moment, we knew God was giving us a gift.

And halfway around the world, my children were in the middle of losing everything they'd once known.

Adoption can be beautiful. But adoption can also be messy. Adoption is full of pain—and full of healing. It's a refining fire that can burn away so much sin and show you how much you need Jesus. Adoption is a beautiful mess that changes every person involved. It's both sweet and sour.

Adoption is necessary because of the world's brokenness. Our children have another mother. They have another father. What loss had our children experienced to bring them to us? They were being grafted into a new family tree because of the loss of their first family. This new growth stemmed from old pain.

Many times since our children came home to us, well-intentioned people have asked some version of this question: "Aren't they so thankful you adopted them?"

I've tried to craft a gracious response, but I'm not sure I've succeeded. The truth is, my children are not thankful they had to be adopted. They are thankful they no longer live in an orphanage, spending every day in a hopeless, monotonous routine. They are thankful not to feel the stabbing pains of hunger or to wonder where their next meal will come from. They are thankful to fall asleep in their warm beds, a place they don't have to worry about hungry hyenas or hungry children prowling in the dark. They are thankful to end each day without having to wonder if their parents will be there in the morning.

But these are things we should all be thankful for: home, family, safety, and food. We should be thankful for these things even if we've never had to go without them. My children have done without, so they are more grateful than most for these everyday blessings. But this does not mean they are thankful to be adopted.

In a January 9, 2015 article in the *Washington Post*, the author, an adult adoptee, addresses this idea that adopted children somehow need to be more grateful than the average person. In *Please Don't Tell Me I Was Lucky to Be Adopted*, Shaaren Pine writes:

Adoption is a traumatic, lifelong experience that is rarely recognized as one.... For me, being an adoptee is like getting into a horrible car accident and surviving with devastating injuries. But instead of anybody acknowledging the trauma of the accident, they tell you that you should feel lucky. Even if the injuries never stop hurting, never quite heal.

My children will never quite heal. They will never stop hurting. My children lost their parents. My future grandchildren lost their grandparents. This loss can never be erased. But it can be remembered, redeemed, and entwined with the beauty of what God is growing in our lives.

And provide for those who grieve in Zion—to bestow on them a crown of beauty instead of ashes, the oil of joy instead of mourning, and a garment of praise instead of a spirit of despair. (Isaiah 61:3 NIV)

None of us make it through life without a few bruises. Some of us have scars that will never quite heal. Some of us are still in triage, daily bandaging our open wounds. Those scars will always be a part of us. While they do not define us, they have played a part in shaping us.

When I hear, "Your children are so lucky to have you. You have changed their lives," my response is always, "I am so lucky to have them. They have changed my life." They changed my life from the moment God whispered to my heart that He had a gift for me. I needed only to reach out my hands and accept it.

As Scott and I gazed into our children's eyes on that computer screen, as we tested their names on our tongues and found them to be sweet, we were planting the first seeds of love in the garden that would be our family. We were clinging tightly to God's promise that He would make beautiful things.

To help plant some of those seeds of hope in our children's hearts, we had the privilege to share with them the news that we were going to be a family. In their years in the orphanage, they had watched as other orphans came and went. They watched as American moms and dads showed up to embrace their Ethiopian children. They watched as the babies, the toddlers, the healthy children, and the singles with no siblings were chosen. They waited for their turn, wondering if and when they, too, might be chosen.

We assembled a package filled with trinkets and bubblegum, stickers and bubbles. We included pictures of our home, their bedrooms, our family. We filled three ziplock bags—one each for Shukriya, Eba, and Eyob—with as much love as we could stuff inside. Then we wrote a letter.

What do you say to introduce yourself to your children? How do you find a way to inspire trust, not fear? How do you convey your hopes, your dreams, and a sense of family to strangers? I am not sure these were the right words, but we tried our best:

To Our Dear Beautiful Children,

We are so excited that you will get to be a part of our family. We have been praying for you for a long time now. The first time we heard your names and saw your pictures, our hearts melted! We can hardly wait to see you and give you a hug! You will love living with us, and we already love you. There is so much we would like to tell you. We can't wait for you to meet your new sister Hannah (she is 7 years old) and your new brother Joel (he is 10 years old). Both of them are so excited to meet you!

We promise that we will always love you and take good care of you. We are so happy that you will be a part of our family. Even though you don't know us yet, we already consider you to be our precious children who we love with all of our hearts. We pray for you every day. We look at your pictures all the time and hope that you are happy and have everything you need. We are working hard to come get you soon and bring you home with us. We promise that we will not leave you there; we will come get you and love you forever.

We live in a small town. We have lots of land for

you to play on and a swimming pool to swim in. We sent you some pictures of us and Joel and Hannah and our house. We know that having a new family is probably scary but do not be afraid. We will always keep you safe and give you what you need and love you and take care of you. You are so special to us and so precious. Together we will be a very happy family. We will have a lot of fun together and will play a lot of games together and watch movies and read books and laugh together a lot. When you are sad we will wipe away your tears and give you hugs and hold you close until you feel better.

We love you so much, our two handsome boys and our beautiful girl. We will never stop loving you. We are coming soon.

Love,
Mommy and Daddy

We filled the spaces between the words with our love and we prayed that our children would feel it. *Read between the lines, children. Do you hear our hearts?* Then we sent it all—our love, our heart, our hopes for our family—across the ocean in a ziplock bag.

We researched airfares, discussed timelines, and pulled out our big suitcases. We expected to leave in two to three weeks to fly to Ethiopia for our court date. We could hardly believe we were so close to becoming a family of seven.

We put pictures on our refrigerator and in our wallets. We proudly showed them to our parents, our friends, and strangers in the grocery store, anyone willing to share in our excitement. When we looked at our future, we could now see our children's faces. We could pray for them by name: Shukriya, Eba, and Eyob.

Then we learned there was another sister.

10

INTO THE STORM

Do snakes poop? I no think so because they no have any bottom."

"Why we change underwear every day, every day, every day? They no dirty!"

Every day my children make me laugh. They are curious, loud, and funny. They can drive me bonkers with their constant questions and demands on my attention. My youngest, in particular, hates silence. He would prefer to have words coming out of his mouth—all day long. He even invented his own game. It involves talking nonstop, of course. In Amharic the word for "or" is *wame* (rhymes with "same"). He likes to play the Wame Game anywhere and everywhere and always.

"Do you like cats better wame dogs?"

"Do you want to go to the beach wame the mountains?"

"Would you rather eat a cookie wame ice cream?" My ears are tired.

The other day when we were running errands, one of my boys had me crying with laughter at his interpretation of the Do Not Walk sign.

"I know what this sign mean, Mom. It mean no wiping your bottom here."

He's right. There is no wiping your bottom on that street corner.

My children are precocious. My children are sweethearts. They are tender, loving, and kind. They make my heart fill with pride as I watch them spread their wings. Last week I cried as I watched one of my boys recite his lines, sing his songs, and present the gospel in a school assembly.

I cried when I got my daughter's report card and saw a line of As and Bs, each representing hours of work, each subject made harder by the fact she is an English-language learner.

I cried when my daughter told me another little girl in her class was being excluded. She invited that girl to join her for lunch.

I cried when my children saw the ocean for the first time. We drove hours over the twisted roads leading to the coast, everyone complaining in the backseat. They had never ridden in a car before we met them and were not accustomed to the restricted space, seat belts pulling against their shoulders, heads made dizzy by the movement of the car.

They fought motion sickness and one another and I seriously doubted the decision to take our first family trip so soon after bringing them home.

Then we pulled up to the state beach and tumbled out of the car. The ocean air blew cool against our skin and the children forgot all about their hours of frustration. We hurried down the fern-lined path and shed our shoes as soon as we hit the beach. We squished sand between our toes and laughed. We walked to the water's edge and the children stared in wide-eyed wonder. We held tightly to their hands and dipped our feet into the water.

Soon we were all chasing waves, allowing the water to splash onto our clothes as we waded deeper. I couldn't wipe the smile off my face as I watched them, laughing, playing, amazed at the power of the ocean.

My daughter followed a wave on its way out to sea and then ran shrieking back toward me as the next wave lapped her heels. She stopped right in front of me, eyes sparkling, as she licked her fingers. "Salt! Mom! It tastes like salt."

Yes, dear. The ocean and my tears.

My children are royalty, children of the King. They are heirs to a legacy of faith. They are strong. They are broken. They are hurt. They are healing. They are overcomers. My children are Ethiopian. They are American. They are part of the family of God. They are orphans. They are sons and daughters. They are complex and beautiful—and they are mine.

I know so much about my children. I know *this* scar came from the time you fell down the hill and a piece of sugarcane stabbed into your leg. Your leg got infected, and you couldn't walk on it for more than a month. Somebody finally removed a piece of cane that was more than three inches long from the wound.

I know *you* are scared of the dark because as you slept on the ground in Ethiopia, you could hear the hyenas all around. To protect yourself from predators of all species, you learned to never venture out after dark.

I know *you* like to play soccer more than anything else and you dream about being a professional player. I know *you* love to sing and dance and perform; you crave the spotlight. I know *you* are uncomfortable being the center of attention and would rather fade into the background, where you feel safe.

My children and I have a relationship. We are family. I cannot separate my role of mother from anything I have come to know about these children. But this wasn't always the case.

When I first heard "They have another sister," all I knew was fear. At that moment, I let *orphan* be the definition, not just a description.

Korean adult adoptee and co-author of *Before You Were Mine: Discovering Your Adopted Child's Lifestory*, Carissa Woodwyk said in a Facebook post:

The word "orphan" is hard for me when it is used (or nuanced) to DEFINE (who someone is) rather than to

DESCRIBE (what's happened in their story). Often times it feels like the "church" is sending the message, "We need to help and rescue the orphans! They are so needy! Look at all that we can do for them! Look at all that we have to give to them!" And this is said, "In the name of Jesus." It feels like US and THEM and that the US are the only ones who are needy and powerless and hopeless and victims. (Which it's true— those who have been orphaned, those who have lost one or both parents, do have very unique and important needs). But, we ALL have needs! It's in our common humanity and through our authentic relationships that a give/receive, 2-way street, mysterious and beautiful thing called "connection" and "healing" can happen— between us and in us. (October 6, 2015)

When we started the adoption process, we knew our children would be orphans. We knew, as Woodwyk said, they would have very specific, important needs. We never expected them to come to us unscathed. But when I heard some of the details about this lost sister's life, I was afraid.

Her past is long and complicated, and it is hers to protect or to share. Her siblings had been living in the orphanage, and they were somewhat prepared to join our family. They had watched similar stories play out as other children and other parents came together. But the older sister had been separated from the rest, sent to work in a stranger's home as a house servant. She was unaware of the events that might rip her from her homeland and move her to a new country and a new family.

When our adoption agency contacted us, they said they had never dealt with a situation like this. They had found an older sister. She was living apart from her siblings in less-than-desirable conditions, but she was not ready or available for adoption.

Our adoption coordinator could not offer us much information. She told us we would have to decide if we wanted to pursue this fourth child. Our agency wasn't sure what that process would look like—or how long it would take. They were not even sure it was possible. They said, "What you do about the sister is completely up to you. You can sign the papers and bring home your three children from the orphanage. Or you can petition the courts and attempt to bring home all four."

Completely up to you.

I wanted to say no.

I really did. From the first time I heard her story, I wanted to say no. I had so many good excuses.

It wouldn't be smart to get involved in another, separate court process. It might affect the timelines for our first three children. It would cost more money. We had no medical history or background for this child. Adoption might not even be possible. We could pour time and money into pursuing her and end up without her. And what about trauma? Who knows what this child had experienced and how that would affect her—or how it would affect our family.

There are always reasons to play it safe rather than step out into the unknown. There are always good excuses for not getting involved in someone else's mess. Their pains and sorrows might rub off on our lives. Their messes might be sticky, hard to navigate, and so dirty our own lives would surely be made dirty.

Inside I was saying, *Three children is enough! If their sister is not available for adoption, then who are we to say otherwise? Also, I'm not good with change. And I'm scared. So no.*

I translated those thoughts into Christianese and said, "We'll pray about it."

Although I was fairly certain God would agree with my assessment of the situation, I had promised to talk to Him about it. I said we'd pray about it, and I meant it. My husband and I committed to spend the weekend in prayer, seeking the Lord's guidance (one of us with a more open heart than the other).

We prayed together, and I read this Bible account about fear:

> *Meanwhile, the boat was far out to sea when the wind came up against them and they were battered by the waves. At about four o'clock in the morning, Jesus came toward them walking on the water. They were scared out of their wits. "A ghost!" they said, crying out in terror. But Jesus was quick to comfort them.*

"Courage, it's me. Don't be afraid." Peter, suddenly bold, said, "Master, if it's really you, call me to come to you on the water." He said, "Come ahead." Jumping out of the boat, Peter walked on the water to Jesus. But when he looked down at the waves churning beneath his feet, he lost his nerve and started to sink. He cried, "Master, save me!" Jesus didn't hesitate. He reached down and grabbed his hand. Then he said, "Faint-heart, what got into you?" (Matthew 14:24–31)

Faint-heart, what got into you?
What was that You called me, God?
Faint-heart.
Yes. That sounds about right.

As we prayed, I felt God move my heart, just as He had time and again during the past year of learning to listen to His voice and trust His plan. He filled my heart so there was no room left for that faintness to hang out.

I realized I wasn't afraid of this child; I was afraid of the unknown. If I were sitting in the same room as this little girl—watching her go hungry; watching her clean house instead of going to school; watching her live without a family, without her sisters and brothers, without a mother and a father—could I really turn away and say no because it might be an inconvenience?

No. I could not turn away.

Then it struck me. No one would ever fault us for adopting three children. People would probably give us all kinds of accolades. They would commend us for traveling halfway around the world to bring these three children into our family. They would never have to know about the child we left behind.

But we would know. In our hearts we would know God had provided this opportunity, and we had turned away.

We presented the idea to our two children. They had been part of the discussion from the beginning. From the first mention of adoption, to following our hearts to Ethiopia, to the commitment to keep a sibling group together—our children had walked with us hand in hand. We were taking these steps of faith together, as a family.

My son Joel had agreed with me when I told Scott that three children was our limit. He is very practical, a trait I greatly admire. When God presented us this opportunity for a fourth child, He also presented us a challenge in the form of my ten-year-old, firstborn child. First God had to change my heart. Then He had to change my son's heart.

We took our son to a coffee shop. We sat across the table from him, eye-to-eye. We told him we valued him and his feelings. We knew any decisions we made would affect our whole family.

Then we introduced him for the first time to his new Ethiopian sister. We explained the circumstances and the challenges we might face. We discussed her situation, and we asked his opinion.

Joel very logically explained why this would be a bad idea. First, he reminded us, we were already worried about money. Didn't we know we would have to buy an extra plane ticket? And we would have to pay more fees, both to the government and to our adoption agency. Besides, we wouldn't all fit into our car! My minivan sat only seven. We couldn't have eight people in our family. We would have to buy a bigger car! And where would she sleep? We didn't have beds for six children.

I understood where Joel was coming from. These were the same arguments I'd been using in my own conversations with God.

We told our son he was right. Logically, none of this made any sense. If we looked only at our circumstances, it would be ridiculous for us to do any of this. We needed to take our eyes off our surroundings and turn them toward Jesus.

Our feelings were like those of the disciples in Matthew 14 when they were in the middle of that storm. Things weren't easy for them out in those deep waters. They were scared. When Jesus showed up in the midst of the storm, at first they didn't recognize Him.

Storms, deep water, fear, not recognizing God's presence. Yes, we had something in common with those disciples.

Despite the circumstances, Peter took a step of faith. He followed Jesus' prompting and stepped out of the boat's safety, into the wind and the waves.

This made no sense. If Peter had weighed the pros and cons of walking on water in the middle of a storm, he would have logically concluded it was not the best move. He would not have stepped out of the boat. He would have stayed where he was: safe, warm, and dry.

God was asking us to step out of our boat. He wanted to see our faith in action. Sometimes we need to obey without understanding how it all will work. We need to step out without having a safety line. Or, more accurately, we need to trust that God will be our safety line. Our actions aren't the victory. Faith is the victory.

We discussed all these things, the three of us in that coffee shop. We asked Joel to pray about it with an open heart and an ear toward God's voice. Nothing more than we asked of ourselves.

This was a test. I'd already had a discussion with God about it. I told Him that while He'd done the work to convince me to pursue this lost child, what I really needed was for Him to do the work in my son's heart. My prayer was "Lord, prepare Joel's heart to receive this news. You need to have him fully endorse this idea." Joel has always had a soft heart toward God. He wants to do the things God has for him.

On that Sunday in the coffee shop, Joel said, "Okay. I'll pray about it. But if you made me decide right now, I would have to say no."

When I checked with him on Monday he said, "I'm still praying about it."

His response on Tuesday: "Mom, I am still praying."

And on Wednesday: "*Mom*, I'll tell you when I am done praying!"

(Somebody around here is impatient. I am sensing a theme.)

I waited until Thursday to ask again. He said, "If you made me decide right now, I would probably say yes."

Finally, on Friday: "You know what? For some reason I think this sister and I are going to be really good friends. I think you should tell our adoption agency we are going to do it. We should go to court and try to bring her home too."

God aced my test. He prepared Joel's heart. Our family was now fully on board with the plans God had laid out for us. Ethiopian siblings. Two boys and two girls. My new children: Hamdiya, Shukriya, Eba, and Eyob.

We were stepping out of the boat without a safety line, and we had no idea of the coming storms. We called our adoption agency and told them we wanted to pursue all four of these children. Of course, they asked for more money.

11

PRICELESS

International travel vaccinations for a family of four: $1,200
Passports and visas for a family of eight: $3,200
Ethiopian lawyer and government fees: $5,000
Adoption agency fees: $30,000
Plane tickets: $15,000
Following God's best plans and reaping the rewards: *priceless*

Those "priceless" credit card ads are so touching. They're designed to focus our attention on the memories and moments we create—and distract us from the reality of the cost. Over here in real life, when the credit card bill comes due and we lack the money to pay it, and the late fees and interest start to add up—it suddenly doesn't feel so priceless.

In our home, I am the spender and my husband is the saver. I am the optimist and my husband is the realist. I am the spice and my husband is the sweet. Some might even say I am the right and he is the wrong. (Okay, maybe I'm the only one who says that.)

Money doesn't particularly concern me, but my husband feels the pressure to provide. That's his role, right? He takes that role very seriously. If our finances aren't happy, he's not happy.

Within the first few weeks of filling out the paperwork with our adoption agency, my husband wanted to sit down with a spreadsheet and figure out how we were going to pay for this adventure. On crunching the numbers, we quickly realized we weren't. For some reason, we didn't have an extra $50,000.

Even if we cut back on spending and didn't buy any more new shoes, heels, wedges, flats, boots, or sandals (a suggestion from my husband, prompted by my membership in a shoe-of-the-month club); borrowed money from our business (my suggestion); and held garage sales and bake sales (our children's suggestion), we still weren't going to come up with enough money.

The night we realized this, my husband had the papers and his spreadsheets scattered across the bed. As the amount we would owe kept growing, his stress level kept rising. He got to the bottom line and threw up his hands. "We can't do this!"

He was right. We couldn't. No matter how he crunched the numbers, we couldn't squeeze out the $30,000 we owed to our adoption agency. He wanted a plan for exactly how we were going to pay. He needed to see it in black and white because our first installment was due. We needed to mail a check the following morning.

There was nothing we could do but pray. We put away the spreadsheets, climbed under the covers, and turned out the lights. We held hands as we prayed together. We asked God to clearly show us we were supposed to go forward in faith, even though we didn't know where the money would come from.

The next morning my husband wrote a check for our deposit. We were stepping out of the boat— something we would have to do over and over in the coming years. He sealed up that check and dropped it into the mailbox. As he did, he prayed that God would provide.

That check was on its way. We had made our commitment and stepped out of the boat. *And then God provided.*

We obeyed. He provided. A very specific order of events. Because sometimes faith is the victory.

As my husband walked away from the mailbox, his phone rang. This might be hard to believe. The timing is too neat and tidy. But sometimes God's provision and timing are so obvious it helps our unbelief.

A lawyer was calling. He just wanted to tell us he was sending us a check for $30,000. (Look back with me at our itemized costs. How much were we going to owe our adoption agency? And how much was this lawyer going to send us? That's right.)

I don't know about you, but it's not every day a lawyer calls to say he's sending us $30,000. And it's not every day we write a check that commits us to stepping out of the boat.

So why would this lawyer send us $30,000? There are two answers: one earthly and one heavenly.

The heavenly answer is that God wanted to use this money not only as His provision, but also as our *Ebenezer*. In 1 Samuel 7:12, the prophet "took a single rock and set it upright between Mizpah and Shen. He named it 'Ebenezer' (Rock of Help), saying, 'This marks the place where God helped us.'"

That $30,000 check was both our Rock of Help and a landmark of the place where God helped us. This practical fulfillment of our immediate needs would also provide a touchstone of remembrance for later, when we were in the middle of the storm. It was proof that we stood right in the middle of the story God had written for us.

The earthly answer is that a legal case had settled. More than five years earlier, Scott had been involved in a car accident. Our insurance company dragged their feet and haggled over the amount they would pay. After months and months, we hired a lawyer. We left all the details in his capable hands. Every few months, the lawyer would call us with an update. He warned us such cases often took years to settle.

Before this Ebenezer moment, we hadn't heard from our lawyer for six months. We had no inkling our case was close to settling. And our lawyer had never mentioned an amount.

But God knew. And He waited to reveal it until the timing was exactly right. He's funny like that. He likes to keep a few tricks up His sleeve to surprise us every now and then.

God gave us $30,000, and we gave it all to our adoption agency. But when we decided to pursue Hamdiya, the older daughter, the costs for our adoption increased. We had no reserves, no backup plan. We were out of the boat with no safety line. But we looked back at our Ebenezer and we knew that if God was calling us to it, God would carry us through.

In February 2012, we accepted the referral for three beautiful Ethiopians.

In March 2012, we answered God's call to pursue a fourth beautiful Ethiopian.

In April 2012, our church family took a love offering for us.

The weekend before the love offering, our pastor asked us how much we needed to complete our adoption. We told him we figured we were only about $20,000 short. No big deal. We asked him to keep that number private. We didn't want to come before our church and ask for a specific amount. We felt that any amount given would help. And we were starting to take God at His word when He said He would provide all of our needs, according to His glorious riches (see Phil. 4:19).

But I was still a little selfish. Just a teeny bit.

During the year of paperwork and preparation, Scott and I had started to fall in love with Ethiopia: its culture, its people, its traditions. We connected with other adoptive families with children from Ethiopia. We got involved with ministries that served there. We tuned our hearts to the special frequency of this beautiful country.

One ministry was in need of blankets. Some products are especially hard to find in Ethiopia, and this ministry asked if we could buy and transport twelve specific blankets for their bunk beds. We said yes.

I kind of wanted to say no. After all, we were in the middle of paying for a big adoption. Every penny was accounted for. We were already busy doing God's work. Surely there was someone else who could provide the blankets. Actually, I know for sure that someone else was available. My friend Jessica offered to pay for the blankets herself. But God wanted me to cover that expense.

I did so, somewhat grudgingly. We bought the

blankets for a total of $300. *(That's $300, God. That's a lot of money when you already need $20,000.)*

God isn't stingy. He's not carefully measuring out a little bit of blessing for this person and just enough to get by for that one. He's not short on resources. He owns the cattle on a thousand hills. He gives gifts that "are rivers of light cascading down from the Father of Light" (James 1:17).

Don't bargain with God. Be direct. Ask for what you need. This isn't a cat-and-mouse, hide-and-seek game we're in. If your child asks for bread, do you trick him with sawdust? If he asks for fish, do you scare him with a live snake on his plate? As bad as you are, you wouldn't think of such a thing. You're at least decent to your own children. So don't you think the God who conceived you in love will be even better? (Matthew 7:7–11)

Okay, then. I'll be direct and ask for what we need.

"God," I prayed, "we need $20,000 and we need it now. We are flying to Ethiopia, and we need to purchase plane tickets. I covered those $300 blankets for You; maybe You could take care of those $20,000 plane tickets for us? But if not, we can go ahead and put it on our credit card."

I'm not kidding. This was my backup plan. I figured that whatever amount was still needed after the love offering would go on my credit card—along with the bill for the $300 blankets.

Remaining adoption expenses: $20,000
Blankets for ministry in Ethiopia: $300
Love offering total: $20,387.54
God proving Himself time after time: *priceless!*

12

<3 U 4EVER

When Scott and I started dating, we talked about traveling the world together. We dreamed of exotic places like Saint Barts, Costa Rica, and Canada. Before getting married, I had been on an airplane only once. I was not what anyone would call a world traveler. To me, Canada sounded pretty exotic. Because my husband loves me, well, on our first anniversary he took me to Canada.

We were broke, so we drove the entire way in our beat-up Ford. We would explore a new place every day, walking the cobblestone streets of Victoria, British Columbia; wandering through the Butchart Gardens; and eating fresh fish dockside in Seattle. We explored gardens in the countryside and street corners in the city. We searched out every free or cheap activity we could find.

One memorable night we tried to go clubbing.

Unfortunately, we had no clubbing experience. We didn't realize there's a certain clubbing look and attitude, neither of which we nailed. This was before my fashion renaissance. Growing up shopping at Goodwill can limit your sense of style. So I wore tennis shoes. And a turtleneck. As we stood in the queue (notice my use of the Canadian word) for a very trendy downtown club, the bouncer would periodically open the gates and allow some to enter. When the bouncer noticed my turtleneck and tennis shoes, he made a beeline straight for me.

He's going to let us skip to the front of the line, I thought. Not exactly. The bouncer said we could leave the queue at any time as there was absolutely no chance of being allowed inside. Thus ended our clubbing experience. We have never fully recovered.

Being broke also meant we couldn't afford a hotel. So we camped every night. We would drive until we found a suitable campsite and pitch our tent. Once we slept on a bluff overlooking the ocean, waves crashing below us. We also slept in a forest of redwoods and ferns. One night we found an open site in a beautiful meadow with a stream running through it. We didn't realize until too late that the meadow was bordered by train tracks. A freight train rumbled past our tent every hour. One memorable night on one of the San Juan Islands, we slept in the back of our car in the middle of a rainstorm. Who knew an old Ford could be so romantic?

Our Canadian vacation was just the first of many. We have since traveled to Mexico and Hawaii, the Caribbean and Panama. And always, we dreamed of traveling to Europe. We told each other we'd celebrate our fifteenth anniversary with a European vacation.

Those European plans were derailed when we decided to follow God's call to adopt. From that point, all of our resources were funneled into this one dream. And we didn't even care. We were so on board with God about this new direction, we never felt like we were giving up anything. We felt like we were gaining. Look at us! What an adventure! This would be even better than our Canadian vacation. Leaving for Africa. Meeting our children. Living in Ethiopia for four months.

The adoption landscape changes constantly. When we were in the midst of it, Ethiopia required two trips for adopting families. During the first trip the family would appear in court and sign the papers making the children legally theirs. The second trip came three to four months later, after the paperwork had cleared and the children had visas and passports for travel to America.

We wanted to live in Ethiopia with our children during the months between their adoption and the completion of their travel paperwork. Wouldn't it be amazing if we could stay with our children while we waited for their visas and passports?

Wouldn't it be fantastic to get to know them in their own country, surrounded by their own people, speaking their own language? Wouldn't it be awesome if they could leave the orphanage on the day they were no longer orphans? We dared to dream those big dreams.

We realize few people could take a four-month sabbatical from their jobs to live overseas. We weren't sure we could do this either. But we were determined to try.

When Scott and I first met, back in high school, only one of us had a job. (One guess as to who was the responsible, hardworking visionary with a plan.) The other one was broke.

This was important because we had all those big travel plans. And more immediately, we wanted to date. But dating for any length of time required some spending money. Scott's parents bankrolled our first few excursions: a picnic and a hike to a waterfall, ice cream sundaes after youth group, one dinner at a nice restaurant. But we quickly realized they wouldn't fund our relationship indefinitely. So I nicely suggested Scott get off his lazy rear end and look for work. He agreed and got a job.

He started working part-time at Apex Technology when he was seventeen. Scott has always been good with computers. He was and still is a technology freak. I, on the other hand, felt I would never need a cell phone, texting, or digital music. I held out on all fronts for far too long, arriving late to the texting party and still running behind on the use of emojis and acronyms.

Scott started as a low-level computer tech, after school and on weekends. He worked part-time all through college. Then, at age twenty-three, with his wife pregnant with their first child, he bought into the company. Perfect timing: Let's have a new baby and a new business! Who needs sleep? This was a *huge* decision for two kids just getting started in life. We had to borrow money. We took out a second mortgage. Scott worked long hours as he learned how to run a technology company.

Over the years Apex has been many things: a three-man shop, a struggling business, an up-and-comer in the local economic landscape, a technology company with integrity, a provider of jobs in our community, and the means God used to allow us to live in Ethiopia for four months while we completed our adoption. Scott was able to take a leave of absence and entrusted the day-to-day decision making to his executive team.

Those four months in Ethiopia were more important than we'd ever imagined. We had hoped to build relationships with our three newest children. Now we knew we'd be fighting for another daughter. Wouldn't it be helpful to have our boots on the ground, doing what was needed to bring her home with us?

Our agency warned us there were no guarantees. Being in the country did not mean we'd be allowed to adopt her. Even if the courts said yes, it might take two years to get her paperwork processed.

We packed her a suitcase anyway. We got our vaccinations, said our good-byes, and packed eight suitcases—one for each member of our family. We found some college kids to stay in our home and care for our dogs. We set up Apex to run as smoothly as possible without Scott. We found a place to stay in Addis Ababa, a guesthouse connected with a ministry we supported. And we purchased our plane tickets for Africa.

Our departure was set for May 18, with our trip including a one-night layover in Germany and arrival in Ethiopia on May 20. One week before we were to leave, we received news that our Ethiopian court date had been canceled. It seemed one piece of paperwork was missing. One single piece of paper. Without that, we wouldn't be able to pass court. Our agency suggested we cancel our tickets until further notice.

We went anyway. We felt this trip was about more than our adoption. It was about the opportunity God had placed before us to work among His people. An opportunity to serve. To step out of our comfort zone in the faith He would provide. Just because we no longer had a firm court date didn't mean we no longer had the opportunity to serve in Ethiopia.

But it did mean we had a flight departing America on May 18, although we didn't have to be in Ethiopia for at least another week. We called the airline and asked how much it would cost to change our one-night layover in Germany to a seven-night layover.

This is how, for only $60, God gave us an anniversary trip in Europe.

Our fifteen-year anniversary was May 24, 2012. We spent that week in Europe, just as we had dreamed of doing all those years ago. We climbed to the top of the Eiffel Tower, took a cruise down the Rhine, toured castles in Germany, and ate beignets in an outdoor café in Paris. And the night of our anniversary, we slept in a castle. (BTW, God, I've always dreamed of spending my twenty-five-year anniversary on a Mediterranean cruise. THX. <3 U 4EVER.)

After our weeklong European anniversary trip, we caught our connecting flight to Ethiopia. Ten hours and thousands of miles later, we arrived in the middle of the night and drove the dark streets to what would be our home for the next few months. We had traveled so far to get here. We had prayed and planned and dreamed, completed hours of paperwork, written checks for money we didn't have, stepped out of the boat, and followed God's call to this unknown place. As we drove the streets of Addis, we looked around at our children's homeland

and realized this was only the beginning. Our family was about to change forever. My first morning in Ethiopia, I wrote these words:

The sights and sounds of Addis are simply overwhelming. Traffic and people and goats and cows all vie for a place on the roadway. The streets are lined with beautiful buildings next door to shacks built out of corrugated metal. Well-dressed businessmen share the street corners with women and children begging with outstretched hands. I saw one man with no legs, his pants pinned up to form a cushion for his body, "walking" down the street on his hands. We have been in this country less than 24 hours, and my feelings are all jumbled. The people here are friendly and beautiful. The need here is immeasurable. And underlying all of this is the constant sense that I am in the same city as my children. They are here. Somewhere. And I will finally get to hold them in my arms on Monday. We are going to meet them for the first time Monday morning. The moment we have been dreaming about and praying for these many months. We are going to begin the journey of knowing these little souls who are about to be a part of our family forever.

13

LABOR PAINS

In my first pregnancy, I had a birth plan prepared by month six. I typed it and presented it to the doctor, the nurses, and various hospital staff. I'll share the highlights. I included such phrases as "instrumental worship music plays softly in the background" and "sits on birthing ball while husband rubs the small of her back." I also specified a eucalyptus candle and "no pain medication."

After my water broke I followed my well-structured, completely naive birth plan for the first fifteen minutes. Then real life got in the way. No one could hear the worship music over my cries of agony. My husband couldn't rub the small of my back because I quickly deleted that rule and replaced it with "You are not allowed to touch me." No medication? Then why did God invent doctors? And pharmacists? And anesthesiologists?

Twenty-six hours after I arrived at the hospital, my birth plan lay in the trash and my son lay in my arms.

The first time I held my newborn, something happened to my heart. Never mind that he was all scrunched up and red, covered in mucus and blood, and I couldn't feel the lower half of my body. Something magical happened. I felt the warm, heavy weight of my child in my arms, I looked down into his eyes, and I suddenly became his mama. We were instantly connected by something bigger than both of us, something otherworldly. It was beautiful and indescribable.

The first time I held my adopted children, something happened to my heart. Never mind that they were stiff and unresponsive, covered in trauma and uncertainty, and I couldn't feel anything but the lump in my throat and the hammering of my heart. Something magical happened. I felt the warm, heavy weight of my children in my arms, I looked down into their eyes, and I suddenly became their mother. We were instantly connected, yet I felt this space between us. We were joined, and at the same time we were separated by something bigger than any of us, something both heartbreaking and lovely. It was beautiful and indescribable.

Beautiful. Indescribable. Heartbreaking. Lovely. Connected. Separated.

Parenting is one giant paradox. Parenting is joy,

and it is pain. It's laughter and tears. Parenting is listening to a tantrum that makes you consider moving to Australia to escape the screaming—and it's standing over your sleeping child and marveling at their absolute perfection.

We equip ourselves for this parenting gig by reading all the manuals and taking all the classes. Then we meet our real-life children and despite all our preparation, we realize we have no idea what we're doing. Maybe we use some "Love and Logic"—to coin a phrase by Jim Fay and Foster W. Cline—to redirect our three-year-old, or maybe we turn on *Sesame Street* to distract them. We are flying by the seat of our pants. No matter. We put on brave faces in front of our kids. We don't want them to know we are making it up as we go along.

As we prepared to meet our Ethiopian children for the first time, we put on brave faces. Inside I was a shaky mess. We were bedraggled, overtired, and overwhelmed. Joel had been having stomach issues, a problem that would plague him for our entire four months in the country. As we drove through town, he leaned out the window and vomited onto the street. Our driver took a wrong turn and we ended up taking the "long way" to the orphanage.

But as I walked through those padlocked gates to meet my children, I was determined to make a good first impression. No crying, overly emotional, dramatic mother here! *Don't worry, new children. I am calm. I am rational. If serenity had a physical identity, you would be looking at her.*

As soon as I saw my children, I started the ugly crying.

They came forward out of the sea of orphans—three beautiful little people, frightened but trying so hard to be brave. They smiled as they let us hug them. I held their little bodies. I kissed their little cheeks. I breathed in their sweet smell. (Okay...maybe *sweet* isn't the right word.) I breathed in their unique smell. They looked at us with uncertain eyes. They giggled as we stumbled through our very limited Amharic.

We spent the afternoon together, all seven of us. Frisbee. Sidewalk chalk. Jump ropes. Kicking a soccer ball. Ordinary, everyday things that would be our building blocks to construct our new family.

The little boys hung from Scott's neck as he gave them horseback rides. They laughed as he bucked them off time and again. The little girls sat side by side as I painted their fingernails. They chose a bright red then held out their hands so everyone could see they matched. Shukriya confiscated my camera and walked around the concrete yard snapping photos. She took more than a hundred pictures. More than eighty were of me.

Me pointing. Me laughing. Me talking.

She examined me through the camera lens, safely at a distance but fascinated with her new mother.

Our children proudly claimed us as their own as they gave us a grand tour of the orphanage. They guarded us closely as we walked the grounds, using their rapid-fire Amharic to reprimand any children who wandered too close. The other orphans trailed at a careful distance, watching and listening and waiting for the day they, too, might meet their new families.

We were led by the hand through the courtyard, home to countless hours of jump rope, hair braiding, and monotony. We saw their classroom, tables pushed too close together in the dim light, paint peeling from the walls behind the faded world map that provided their first glimpse of America. We saw their shower station, a rain barrel where they lined up once a week for their turn for a sponge bath. We saw their bedroom, lined end to end with bunks, one blanket per child, and no one to tuck them in or watch over them as they slept. In the months to come we would hear stories about our children taking shifts, each one sleeping in turn, then waking up to be watchful in the dark of the night.

We sat on the covered porch, the one place in the orphanage with a couch. It was reserved for families like ours, families spending their first moments together. We pulled our children onto our laps, all seven of us piling on the couch. We talked softly and haltingly about their new home. We showed them pictures of the empty bedrooms waiting to be filled.

The backyard with the pool where they would learn to swim. Their new grandparents, aunts and uncles, and cousins—unfamiliar faces and names who were now forever written into their story line. We offered an overview of a life that was completely foreign but that would one day become safe, familiar, and filled with the security of love.

We found someone to take our picture, the first of our new family. This picture hangs on our wall today, a reminder of God's promise to create beauty from the ashes: a family, pieced together from different countries, different histories, and different skin tones, huddling in an orphanage courtyard.

Then it was time to leave. We gathered our children in close and explained we would be back the next day. And the next, and the next, and the next. We promised we would come again and again until the day they were allowed to walk out of those gates with us. We said good-bye. They called Joel *brother*. They called Hannah *sister*. They said, "Tomorrow, Mama?" We told them we loved them: words they were not used to hearing but words we hoped would imprint upon their hearts. We hugged our children tightly, then we got into our van and drove away.

We had shared our first moments as a family, the first of many. We had begun the hard work of creating a new normal, for them and for us. It wouldn't form instantly, this bond we were forging. When I held my newborns in my arms for the first time, it was suddenly *us* instead of *me*. But it was different with my adopted children. We were not the beginning of their stories. Their stories began years ago, in a hut on the outskirts of a rural village. They each carried a lifetime of experiences and memories that did not include me. We had to find a way to honor those memories while we created new ones. We had to build bridges from the past to their future.

Those bridges would be built with time, with love, and with the help of the Master Builder. He builds the strongest bridges. He designs the most amazing families. He binds up the brokenhearted.

14

"I CHOOSE YOU"

So don't be afraid: I'm with you. I'll round up all your scattered children, pull them in from east and west. I'll send orders north and south: "Send them back. Return my sons from distant lands, my daughters from faraway places. I want them back, every last one who bears my name, every man, woman, and child whom I created for my glory, yes, personally formed and made each one." (Isaiah 43:5–7)

My children were scattered and separated. Three lived in the orphanage. Two lived with me in the guesthouse. One lived in a rural village on the edge of Ethiopia.

My oldest daughter has a story all her own. Hamdiya had been sent to live with another family, far away from where she was born. She was treated as a sort of house servant, required to do the most menial tasks, sleep on the floor, and take care of the family. She was isolated. She was scared. She was lonely. But she was never alone.

God was there with her.

Then God brought her to me.

For her adoption to be possible, the courts said she must be returned to her mother. Then her mother must relinquish her to a government orphanage. Once the orphanage had Hamdiya in their care, they would begin the required paperwork for adoption. In Ethiopia, this paperwork takes one year to complete.

I made another list.

Step one: Hamdiya is released from her servitude and returns to her mother.
Step two: Hamdiya's mother relinquishes her to the orphanage.
Step three: Paperwork.
Step four: Adoption.

Our agency estimated this process would take two years. We had two months.

God told me He would gather up my children. He said He would "round them up," "pull them in," and "return" my sons and daughters from distant lands. Those are strong words. God wasn't going to sit around and leave my children in those faraway places. He'd made a promise.

Scott flew to Harer, the area where our children lived before they entered the orphanage. Step one had already been completed. Hamdiya had returned home. I checked that off my list and was ready to start on step two.

But the orphanages in Ethiopia are overcrowded. The government orphanage in Harer had turned her away, saying they had no room, no beds, no food, for even one more orphan. Our daughter was left in limbo, living with the mother who would be relinquishing her, waiting for the mother who would claim her. This tension, living in the space between two mothers, would prove to be a place filled with pain.

Our children have two mothers. Both mothers are alive and living worlds away from each other. Both mothers love their children.

Every mother, regardless of her circumstances, has a connection to the children she births. If one of those children is gone, then a piece of her heart is missing.

And every child, regardless of their circumstances, has a connection to the woman in whose womb they were formed. If that mother is gone, then a piece of the child's identity is missing.

My children are missing a piece of their identity.

As Jody Landers, adoption advocate and cofounder of the Adventure Project, says, "Children born to another woman call me 'mom.' The magnitude of that tragedy and the depth of that privilege are not lost on me."

Parenting my children is a privilege I have been granted only because of the magnitude of tragedy they have experienced.

In the classification of orphans, our children are not true double orphans. How heartbreaking that the number of orphaned children is so great, there's a classification system! True orphans, double orphans, maternal orphans, paternal orphans, orphans of poverty, voluntarily relinquished, removed from the home. Belonging to one group does not quantify a child's pain or their need. It simply identifies their loss.

That our children are not true double orphans in no way diminishes the fact they lost their mother. She may be alive and loving them from afar, but they are lost to one another. They are separated by a host of factors too raw and personal to share. Death might have been an easier way to separate. Death is final. There is no second-guessing of motives. There is no wondering about the depth of love. There is no questioning, "If my mother loved me, why did she give me away?" There is no rejecting of one mother to prove allegiance to the other.

Death doesn't create the kinds of memories that linger in the shadows of our children's psyches, ready to taint any good thing with the bitterness of rejection. The kind of memories that whisper, "You are not wanted." For when the orphanage finds room, and your mother says good-bye and walks away, your understanding of your mother is reframed. Pieces of you are broken in ways that can never be repaired.

And when your new mother tries to pick up those broken pieces, she finds them sharp and painful. They cut through her good intentions and her hope for quick healing. Whenever I brush up against them, those jagged edges cut a little bit deeper. Those broken pieces make me bleed.

If I could have glimpsed the years of rejection that awaited me, if I could have felt then the pain from the wounds I would receive as my oldest daughter and I battled together through this minefield, would I have continued down this path? Would I have fought as hard and prayed as fervently for her to join our family?

Yes. A thousand times yes.

I know this is the correct answer, the words I would want my daughter to see if she were ever to read these pages. But it is also the truth.

Leah Hamdiya, there is something I want you to know. I have something to say to you, from a mother to her cherished daughter: I chose you then. I choose you now. You are chosen.

I would choose you over and over again, even knowing what I do now. *Especially* knowing what I do now. Now that I know you, how could I choose a life that didn't include you? Yes, you're right when you roll your eyes and say, "Mom, you don't know everything. You can't see inside my head." I don't know everything about you. But I know enough. I know you like to sing and dance and laugh. I know you worry you aren't good enough. You are, my darling. You are good enough. I know you love God with a fierceness I admire. I know you are driven and dedicated, and if ever there was an overcomer, you are one.

I know you are most comfortable when you can control your emotions, so you keep them under lock and key until they get too big for that confined space and spill into everyday life. I know the feel of your silky curls as I run my fingers through them. I know you fit perfectly against me, tucked under my chin and close to my heart.

I know we spent a lot of our yesterdays apart, but together we will face all of our tomorrows. I found this poem. I wish I had written it for you, but I can't take the credit. I feel these words as if they were my own. And I hope that you can feel them too.

Legacy of an Adopted Child

Once there were two women
Who never knew each other.
One you only remember,
The other you call Mother.
Two different lives
Shaped to make yours one.
One became your guiding star;

The other became your sun.
The first gave you life;
And the second taught you to live it.
The first gave you a need for love;
And the second was there to give it.
One gave you a nationality;
The other gave you a name.
One gave you a seed of talent;
The other gave you an aim.
One gave you emotions;
The other calmed your fears.
One saw your first sweet smile;
The other dried your tears.
One gave you up—
It was all that she could do.
The other prayed for a child,
And God led her straight to you.
And now you ask me,
Through your tears,
The age-old question
Through the years:
Heredity or environment
Which are you the product of?
Neither, my darling—neither,
Just two different kinds of love.

—Author unknown

Sweetheart, you are the product of so much love.
God formed you in one mother's womb and joined

you to another mother's heart. He knows everything there is to know about you, and He loves every single part of you. As do I, my daughter. And while your other mother is not here to tell you, I know beyond a shadow of a doubt that she loves you too.

15

"TOGETHERISING"

According to a 2016 UNICEF report:

- 3 million children worldwide die from malnutrition and starvation every year;
- 36.7 million people live with HIV;
- 25.8 million of those who are HIV-positive live in sub-Saharan Africa;
- 385 million children live in extreme poverty;
- 140 million children are orphans.

The statistics are overwhelming. The numbers represent a mountain of misery. I could never move that mountain. While I am willing to dig in and get dirty, I have only a teaspoon with which to work.

Because the idea of moving that mountain with a teaspoon is so daunting, I and others throw up our hands in defeat. We anesthetize ourselves with Starbucks and Facebook, finding it easy to rationalize our lack of involvement by blaming the size of the problem.

I say, let's pick up our teaspoons and get busy.

No, I cannot eliminate the entire mountain. But my little teaspoon can move at least one molehill.

And what if you joined me? If you picked up your teaspoon and I picked up mine and we worked side by side. What if we began "togetherising"?

Author and activist Glennon Doyle Melton coined the term. She started a foundation, a coalition of women who support other women. Glennon calls her foundation Together Rising. The first time I read the term, I claimed it as my own. I like to imagine I invented *togetherising*. (Also the word *kumquat*...it's so quirky and sweet, just like the fruit itself. It seems perfect to describe my children. I use it often as a pet name for my little kumquats.)

Melton declares togetherising to be as much about the GIVERS as it is about the RECEIVERS. When we are a giver, we rise. When we are a receiver, we rise. We will be both givers and receivers at different times throughout our life. It does not matter which we are; it matters only that we participate. We give. We receive. We rise together.

I declare *togetherise* to be a verb. It is actively *being* together, *being* supportive, and *being* empathetic—

with our colaborers and the ones we are laboring to serve. *Togetherising* is *being* community, coming alongside one another and working toward a common goal.

Togetherising is what you do when someone shares with you the deepest parts of her heart, her secret fear and shame, and instead of offering solutions you simply join with her in her pain. I am "togetherising" with you, you say.

What if more people started togetherising? What if you and I and our neighbors and our friends and our enemies began togetherising? If we all picked up our teaspoons and started digging, that mountain of misery would shrink day by day by day, one teaspoon at a time.

While we were in Ethiopia, we determined to use our teaspoons to the best of our abilities. This meant not only fighting for Hamdiya, but also fighting for her country, her people, and her heritage.

Scott started by beating down doors to quicken the estimated two-year process. He hired a translator and drove from courthouse to magistrate to orphanage to lawyer's office, gathering signatures. I could fill pages with the miracles we experienced.

The day we needed a judge's signature to file a particularly important document, Scott arrived at the courthouse to be told the judge was on vacation for three weeks. But our translator knew where this judge lived. We drove to her house, Scott knocked on her door, and five minutes later we left with her signature.

Or the time Scott went to the courthouse to get a packet of paperwork that had been filed three months earlier, when we first found out about our bonus child. But the courthouse had misplaced this packet. It was nowhere to be found.

Scott was told they would have to redo the entire thing, adding three months to our timeline. But as he was leaving, a secretary stopped my husband in the hallway. It seems that out of the hundreds of documents that cross her desk, she remembered ours. Because our bonus child has such a distinctive name, the secretary had decided to make a copy. "Wait just a moment, sir. I do believe I kept that copy in my desk. Oh, yes. Here it is. Go ahead and take it with you." More proof of God's miraculous work.

While we had only teaspoons, we knew Someone who had a shovel. Or maybe a backhoe. Or a bulldozer. I'm not good with machinery, but you get my drift. God doesn't work with just a teaspoon. He pulls out the big equipment when needed. He provides the miracles. Although He could move the mountain on His own, He likes us to work alongside. To join Him, teaspoons and bulldozers working in harmony. Communicating. Trusting. Togetherising with God. There's no one better with whom to togetherise.

As we dug furiously toward a future with our daughter, we were also digging at the mountain of misery that exists in the country that will always be a part of her past.

We togetherised with Bring Love In, a ministry creating new families from widows and orphans. We did a little bit of everything: sorted donated clothing, refinished tables and chairs, installed a washing machine. We checked off a long list of menial tasks, ones ideally suited for people with teaspoons like ours.

On a Monday in June we found ourselves inside a huge warehouse that had been transformed into a dental clinic for the day, staffed by a traveling team of nurses and doctors. A rudimentary receptionist's desk tracked and distributed the patients, depending on their dental needs. A line of people willing to wait for hours snaked out the door and around the block.

That day it was raining. People leaned against the buildings and waited on street corners in the mud. The endless waiting, the flimsy plastic chairs, dim lighting, lack of anesthesia—nothing deterred the throngs of people. With my lack of medical knowledge and squeamish stomach I felt ill-equipped. All I could do was sit in one of the chairs and hold the hand of a man who needed a crumbling, decaying tooth pulled. During nearly two hours of oral surgery, bits of bone and blood dribbled down his chin. There was no deadening medication. So he squeezed my hand in silence. When it was over I gave him a handful of ibuprofen and a hug. That's how I used my teaspoon.

We spent a day in Kechene Care Point on the outskirts of Addis Ababa, visiting the child we have sponsored for years. We toured her school, met all the students, and listened to a hundred schoolchildren's voices joined in worship. The song was their gift to us. We handed out bracelets, stickers, and packs of gum. We drove to the local market and filled our van with bananas, mangoes, pineapples, and bread. That day we used our teaspoon to feed a schoolful of beautiful children.

We traveled to southern Ethiopia to the town of Sodo. Do you realize there is not one heart surgeon in all of Ethiopia? And not one dialysis machine? But one hospital serves the sick and downtrodden of rural Ethiopia. Soddo Christian Hospital is staffed by a mix of overseas missionaries and local men and women, togetherising every day as they minister to those wounded in body and spirit. At this rural hospital, Scott learned of their IT needs. We spent a week on-site, building their network, servicing their equipment, and running their cabling. We used our teaspoon to provide technology solutions to a hospital in rural Ethiopia. A hospital full of people without health, but not without hope.

I began togetherising with a group of local women, teaching Zumba at a gym in the heart of the capital city. Along with mothering, writing, laundering, and list-making, teaching Zumba is something I do well. I also teach other formats of fitness classes. I never imagined that God could use this talent in His kingdom.

I found a gym in Addis Ababa, offered to teach classes, and suddenly I had a room of twenty-five Ethiopian women showing up to spend time with me. They didn't speak English and I certainly didn't speak Amharic, but we communicated. There was a lot of dancing, a lot of sweating, and a whole lot of smiling. We togetherised ourselves, and I used my teaspoon to build relationships.

We togetherised with many of our friends from home as we collected funds for the government orphanage in Harer. The orphanage in Addis Ababa, where our other three children lived, was far from ideal, but it was privately owned and provided the basics. The government orphanage in Harer, however, had *no* diapers, *no* medicine, and a very meager supply of food. We published a plea for donations on our blog, and our friends picked up their teaspoons. We raised enough money to stock the entire supply closet, every shelf full to overflowing. Many, many people used their teaspoons to fill hungry bellies and cover naked baby bottoms in that government orphanage.

The orphanage with the newly filled supply closet was the one to which Hamdiya had been relinquished. The first time Scott had traveled there to advance her paperwork and spend time with her, he'd been appalled. This was where our older daughter would be staying for an undetermined period of time. We could not sit idly by and leave her in those conditions. We could not leave any precious children in those conditions. Hamdiya was just one face among many, each of them hungry, naked, or sick. Each one without a family. There are 4.6 million orphans in Ethiopia. That number is overwhelming. What can be done?

Pick up our teaspoons. That's all we can do. We all have different teaspoons, so this looks different for each of us. As Paul says in 1 Corinthians, "There are different kinds of spiritual gifts, but the same Spirit is the source of them all. There are different kinds of service, but we serve the same Lord. God works in different ways, but it is the same God who does the work in all of us" (12:4–6 NLT).

You might use your teaspoon to fill an empty supply closet. Maybe your friend uses hers to sponsor a child. Your neighbor uses his to scrub toilets at a homeless shelter. I used mine to scoop up four of those orphans and make them my sons and daughters.

So now that's 4.6 million minus four.

It may not seem that number changed by much, but for us, everything changed.

TEASPOONS NEEDED

Here is a list of ministries and organizations. Some of these we worked with in Ethiopia, others we have supported at other times and in other ways. Consider these opportunities for you to pick up your teaspoon. Don't be afraid to dig in and get dirty.

Lifesong for Orphans—Bringing joy and purpose to orphans through in-country orphan care, church partnerships, adoption funding, and foster care outreaches.
www.lifesongfororphans.org
PO Box 40
Gridley, IL 61744
309-747-4527

Bring Love In—Creating new families from widows and orphans in Ethiopia
www.bringlove.in
PO Box 1063
Cedar Park, TX 78630
347-669-0125

Ordinary Hero—Changing the world for one today
www.ordinaryhero.org
PO Box 1945
Brentwood, TN 37024
803-470-HERO

World Vision—Building a better world for children
www.worldvision.org
PO Box 9716
Federal Way, WA 98063
888-511-6548

Soddo Christian Hospital—Using new technologies
to provide excellent care
www.soddo.org
Soddo Christian Hospital
PO Box 305
Sodo, Wolaita, Ethiopia

St. Luke's Health Care Foundation
PO Box 4465
Wheaton, IL 60189-4465
630-510-2222

Together Rising—Together is better
www.togetherrising.org
800 West Broad Street, #6409
Falls Church, VA 22040

16

"TIA"

When we traveled to Ethiopia we had to reset our body clocks. The first night of our European layover found our family awake at two in the morning, wandering the streets of Germany in search of breakfast food. All the cafés were closed, with the daily specials in every window showing some variation of sausage and beer. We finally found an open McDonald's and ate several orders of french fries inside a surprisingly crowded restaurant. Judging by the average age and attire of those around us, I would guess that those wandering the streets of that German city at 2:00 a.m. were more into the party scene than our family of four.

We never went back to sleep that night, instead catching a thirty-minute nap the next afternoon that held us until bedtime. I was proud of my children, who handled their jet lag and the time change like seasoned travelers.

The people of Ethiopia not only live ten hours ahead of California time, they also count their hours differently. What we would call 6:00 a.m. in California would be considered one o'clock in Ethiopia. They begin a day's hours when the sun rises. They eat breakfast around 2:00, lunch at 7:00, and dinner between 12:00 and 13:00. Bedtime is around 17:00, and the next morning when you wake up, everything starts over at 1:00.

The years run differently too. As I write these words it is 2015 in most of the world. But in Ethiopia it's 2007. Although today is May 31 in my living room in California, in Ethiopia it is May 23. This made for some interesting issues when translating paperwork between English and Amharic. All the dates also had to be translated.

Living in Ethiopia changed our perspective on time. There's a saying we adopted to describe many of our frustrations—the traffic congestion that made a fifteen-mile commute across town take two hours, the questionable mail delivery, the continual court delays, the constant rescheduling of appointments. We said "TIA"—This is Africa. The catchall phrase describes what Americans might feel is a lack of punctuality, but what Africans attribute to a pace of life that focuses more on people than on tasks. When they say *today*, it might really mean today. Or it might mean tomorrow. Or maybe next week.

The upside is that people take time for one another. If you have an appointment but your neighbor invites you in for a coffee ceremony, you have coffee. The appointment can wait. People come first. You rarely see anyone rushing from one overscheduled activity to another. Instead, they take time to talk and laugh and visit. When you greet someone, instead of an impersonal "Hey!" as you move on by, people stop, clasp hands, and kiss each other's cheeks...three or four times. Left cheek, right cheek, left cheek, right cheek.

The downside at the time was that we had been living in Ethiopia for seven weeks and the courts had not finalized our adoptions. Four of our children were still living in orphanages, and it was time to have them home with us.

Every day of those seven weeks, we had either emailed or gone in person to the local adoption agency office. Every single day. I think people were getting tired of us. I *know* people were getting tired of us. We were getting tired of ourselves. With our persistence and extreme tunnel vision, we were slightly annoying. We were worn down by all the fighting for paperwork. We were ready to be a family.

The adoption court in Addis refused to finalize the adoption of Shukriya, Eba, and Eyob until they tracked down one missing document. One stinking document. Everything else was in place! But for seven weeks the judge waited on a document that needed to come from the courts in Harer.

The courts in Harer refused to generate this document. We put our foot down. If we could be persistent and annoying in Addis, then we could just as easily be persistent and annoying in Harer. Scott flew there again. We decided he should get the document himself. And he could use the time to visit Hamdiya and possibly make more progress on her case.

Again he hired a translator and got to work. He pounded on doors and camped outside the judge's quarters. He traveled the dusty streets from morning 'til night, barely stopping to eat or rest.

He did carve out the time to take Hamdiya on her first daddy-daughter date, springing her from the orphanage for one evening and taking her to dinner and a show. By *dinner* I mean they sat on the ground around a campfire on the outskirts of the village and ate with their hands. And by *show* I mean they watched the locals feed the hyenas who crept through the holes in the walls every night. It was quite the production, hooking raw meat onto the end of long sticks and enticing the hyenas to come close enough to see their eyes glow in the firelight.

Hamdiya remembers this night fondly, speaking of her excitement and nervousness as she spent time with a man she barely knew, a man who would become her father. She now tells me that although they could not understand each other, she knew he was kind. She could tell by looking in his eyes.

The day after the hyena feeding, the director of the Harer orphanage called Scott into his office. He had a proposition. He had several orphans who needed to be moved to Addis Ababa. This was a journey of twelve hours on winding, narrow roads. For the orphanage it was an expensive trip—paying for a driver and a bus, two days of travel time, and food for the children while they were on the road.

If Scott would finance the journey and be ready to leave by the next morning, the orphanage director would sign all the required paperwork to release Hamdiya from his care. She would be allowed to move to the orphanage in Addis where her siblings were staying.

Scott called me from Harer that night with the news that he would be coming back to Addis sooner than expected. He wasn't catching his return flight; rather, he would arrive in a bus filled with orphans. Well, a bus filled with orphans and one very special daughter.

TIA. This is Africa. A land of the unexpected. A place where I learned not to focus on my frustrations with Ethiopian time, but to trust in the perfection of heavenly time. Elisabeth Elliot wrote, "I don't know, when I'm asking for something here on earth, what is going on in the innermost shrine of Heaven (I like to think about it, though). I am sure of one thing: it is good."

The innermost shrine of heaven scheduled this for us. And it was good. So very, very good. Scott arrived in Addis the next day, and he brought our daughter with him.

Hamdiya had not seen her siblings for several years. They had been separated by time and distance and circumstance—Hamdiya living in servitude and her siblings living in the orphanage. During those years, Shukriya would pray every night while she lay in her bed. Huddled under a single blanket, awake and alert for her shift on guard against the evils of the night, she would spend time with God. Every night she prayed she might see her sister again.

God answered her prayers. He reunited brothers and sisters, He provided the orphaned with a new mother and father, and He gave me new children.

The courts signed the adoption decree.

After seven weeks of waiting, on a random Wednesday afternoon in Ethiopia, the judge looked over our paperwork one more time. She sat in her office and reviewed our case. We were not on her docket for the day. She had not received the missing document. Nothing had changed. But for some reason when she checked our file on this Wednesday afternoon, she decided to finalize our adoption—without the missing document. No fanfare. No advance notice. No reason. No more waiting.

TIA. This is Africa. And even in Africa, *especially* in Africa, God's timing rules supreme.

We received a phone call from the judge telling us we were a family. On that Wednesday afternoon, July 4, 2012, we got the news we had been waiting for.

The Fourth of July. Independence Day. Freedom had been granted to us all. Freedom from our past. Freedom to face the future together. Freedom from our circumstances. Freedom from waiting. Freedom that comes only from the One who holds our lives and times in His hands.

On July 4, 2012, we became a family full of hope and promises. A family full of freedom.

We drove to the orphanage for the last time. We fulfilled the promise we had made many weeks ago to our children before we walked out of those padlocked steel gates. No more saying our good-byes at the end of every afternoon.

Instead, we said good-bye to a life lived under lock and key. We said good-bye to their sleepless nights with no one to tuck them in or pray over them as they slept. We said our good-byes to the nannies and the friends and the memories our children had made in that place.

We took our children home with us.

We stood them in the shower and let warm water run down their bodies. We scrubbed little feet and massaged conditioner into curly hair. We wrapped them in clean towels and clothed them in fresh-smelling pajamas. We stood them in front of the bathroom sink and showed how to brush their teeth. Then we tucked them into bed for the first time.

Damp heads rested on soft pillows. Quiet giggles came from the darkened bedrooms. Brothers and sisters lay together, tucked under the comforter. And I sat on the end of the bed and said the prayer I've had the privilege to pray over my children every single night they have been in my care. Joel and Hannah had heard it every night of their lives. And now my newest children would be a part of the same prayer of protection.

The Lord bless you and keep you
The Lord make His face to shine upon you
The Lord be gracious unto you and give you
    great peace.

This is more than a bedtime prayer. It's a prayer over my children's lives. A prayer of promise and hope. A prayer of peace.

I kissed their foreheads and watched them close their eyes. I waited until they drifted off to sleep before I left their side. I lay in bed that night thanking God for giving us this first day together as a family. The first day of our forever.

The threads of our lives had been irrevocably woven together. Our family tapestry forever expanded. That night, I had a glimpse of the future. A look down on our tapestry from above. The vast sweeping colors, the bold shapes, the beautiful designs God was creating with our lives. It was breathtaking.

But every tapestry has an underside. Turn it over and you find the dangling threads, the knots, and the mess. You can't see God's masterpiece when you view it from the bottom. It looks like a jumbled confusion of color with no rhyme or reason.

Over the months and years to come, I would revisit time and again this image of a tapestry. I would remind myself that God had designed and created it, so it could be nothing short of beautiful. I needed that reminder because often, from down here looking up, all I could see was the mess.

17

COLORED

Our earliest family memories are colored by the beauty of Ethiopia. The deep green of ripening crops. The dusty brown of barren fields. The pale blue of endless skies. The colors and flavors of Ethiopia are a part of our family forever. We had the privilege of living in my children's homeland for four months. We formed our first attachments while surrounded by the sights, smells, and sounds that meant home to them. Many of our early days were spent in the orphanage courtyard. We were there every afternoon. We would visit between the hours of one and three. This was when the other orphans were all confined to their beds for nap time. Our children were allowed the great freedom of skipping their naps and instead playing with their parents. We strung those stolen minutes together like brightly colored beads: giving piggyback rides, kicking a soccer ball, and waiting for the courts to release the children to our care.

Our first shared meal was something our children had grown up eating: injera, shiro, dinich wot. They demonstrated how to use the sour pancake-like bread to scoop up the vegetable stew. How to fold it in on itself and minimize the waste. How to eat without utensils, relying on fingers to get the job done.

Our first outing was to a coffee shop. Ethiopia is the birthplace of coffee, after all, and the Ethiopian people take this honor seriously. You can get a good cup of coffee on every street corner: strong, dark, and hot. We were granted permission to take our children out of the orphanage and found a little coffee shop that served ice cream. We watched as they stared wide-eyed at the glass display case. We helped them choose a flavor and then laughed at their expressions when they tasted the sweet, cold treat for the first time.

We organized a little field trip to a local hotel. There are only two hotels with pools in all of Addis. We paid the day-pass fee and introduced our children to the joys of swimming. We applied sunscreen, slid on their water wings, and eased them into the shallow end. They held tight to our necks at first, but they were eventually splashing and playing like pros.

We quickly learned the Amharic word for "wait" and "enough" as we juggled multiple children who were not used to the structure of a family. We also learned to interpret their often-repeated gesture: a quick shoulder shrug and a face turned away. This was their way of defying us, shrugging off our rules and authority.

After the adoption decree had been signed, we were released from the restrictions placed on us by the orphanage. We had officially become a family, and we no longer confined our relationship to between the hours of one and three. We expanded our horizons.

I excitedly planned our first full-day excursion as a family of eight. We hired a driver and took the kids to the mall. The streets of Addis are congested, full of cars and pedestrians and livestock. Goats walk down the middle of the road, weaving in and out of traffic. Bajaj motorcycle taxis dart through the traffic with seemingly no concern for life or limb. There is noise everywhere: the honking of horns, the braying of donkeys, the calls of street vendors, and the bustle of crowded sidewalks. You have to hold tightly to the person next to you or risk being parted and swallowed up.

As we pushed our way through the crowds I was constantly counting little heads to make sure I hadn't lost a child in the press of people around me. I attempted to explain in broken English and hand gestures that my children needed to stay close. Our youngest in particular had no strong attachment to us and no great fear of being separated from us. Our connection was too new to have a hold on him yet.

We slowly made our way to an arcade on the top floor of the mall. We bought tokens and divided them among six outstretched hands. As we rode the go-karts, climbed through the nets and raced down the slides of the obstacle course, and lifted our children onto the brightly colored horses on the carousel, I became acutely aware of the dark faces around me. We were the only white people in the entire arcade. Everyone else shared a common skin color and a common language. We were the outsiders. My children were more a part of them than of me.

I was distracted by my doubts. What were these people thinking about me, a white mother adopting four of their own children? Did they look on me with contempt? Would they assume I was going to snatch these children from their homeland and strip away their heritage? Did they fear I wouldn't know how to properly care for their beautiful black curls? I feared the same thing myself.

Parenting black children was about to make me more aware of race than I had ever been before. It forced me to examine my worldview and brought me face-to-face with beliefs I didn't even know I had. When asked directly, most people would adamantly deny they are racist. Maybe "racist" is too harsh a term. It immediately throws up walls of defense and leaves the person unable to truly examine themselves. Maybe a better term would be "unac-knowledged bias." White privilege.

We all have a lens through which we view the world. This lens is shaped by childhood, parents, environment, and heredity. It is shaped by culture, country, the media, textbooks, teachers, and friends. We wear glasses that interpret the world through the perspectives we have accepted.

If we are white, and we have lived in a predominantly white community, our glasses have been shaped by white perspectives.

If we are black, and we have lived in a predominantly black community, our glasses have been shaped by black perspectives.

It is hard to look through another's glasses. The prescription doesn't feel quite right. Everything we once thought was clear suddenly becomes blurry and we see shades of gray.

I have worn white-colored glasses my entire life. Now I was parenting children whose world looked much different from mine. I needed to reexamine everything through their eyes.

Why, when we stroll through the toy section of Target, is the aisle lined with baby dolls that look like me?

Why, when my son scraped his knee, did I apply a Band-Aid that matched my skin tone, not his?

Why had I never noticed before that our pediatrician, dentist, and school principal all wore the same-colored glasses I did? Where were the people in respected positions with skin that matched my children's?

Our white perspective is so deeply a part of us that it is unacknowledged and ignored. In fact, many people deny it even exists.

So why, in a waiting room full of strangers, did an older gentleman turn and ask my daughter, "Do you know John Smith? He is a colored pastor here in town."

And why, when a well-meaning adoption advocate was patting my back and saying how wonderful it was we had adopted four children, did she also add, "My brother had seven foster children. He ended up adopting five of them, even the littlest one who was black."

Why, in the hallways of our church, did one of the children's workers ask, "You are adopting from Africa? Do they test for AIDS before they send the kids to you?"

And why, in a 2003 study conducted by the National Bureau of Economic Research, did white-sounding names receive 50 percent more callbacks for interviews? Same application, same résumé, different names. The stereotypical African-sounding names (Jamal, Lakisha) received less than half of the positive responses.

These are the kinds of things white glasses filter out. I am working hard to wipe the white smudges off my glasses. I don't want to live a filtered life. I want to see the world in Technicolor. I want the same thing for my children. And for you.

Skin color was only one issue of many that made me question myself. Skin. Hair. Language. So many unknowns. Was I equipped to parent these children?

I watched my son play a video game for the very first time. He was completely absorbed in the virtual world, driving the race car with his entire body. Leaning to the left as he took a turn at full speed. I laughed at his enthusiasm and wondered if I would be enough for him.

And then, as we stood in line to buy Coca-Colas, pressing the cold glass bottles into sweaty palms, a woman stepped up behind me. She spoke in heavily accented English as she asked, "Are these all your children? Did you adopt these four?"

My heart stuttered as I turned to look at her. Just as I had thought. People had been staring at me all day. One of them had finally found the nerve to approach me.

"Yes," I told her. "Yes, we adopted these four. Yes, these are my children."

She reached out and grasped my hand. "Thank you," she said. "Thank you for doing this. Thank you for giving these children a home. This is a wonderful thing." She turned her gaze on the six children standing in front of us. She stood shoulder-to-shoulder with me as we looked at our children. Her nationality, my family, blended together. I gathered strength from her quiet presence. I felt a solidarity with her, this unknown woman in a foreign country who was now standing beside me.

That woman in the arcade gave me a boost of confidence I would desperately need in the coming weeks as my authority and confidence were challenged again and again. Building a family from so many broken pieces was hard work. We needed help and encouragement along the way.

We hired a language teacher. He came to the house three times a week. We sat around the table as he introduced basic English and Amharic words, giving us the tools we would need to communicate with one another. These lessons quickly turned into therapy sessions as he acted as interpreter. That kitchen table was where we first learned our oldest daughter was staging a coup.

She had come late to the party, as it were. We had been spending time with our other children for months by the time she joined our family. She didn't know us. She didn't trust us. She wanted to protect her sister and brothers from hurt and rejection, the inevitable result of every relationship she had so far experienced in life. Our teacher/interpreter translated her words for us.

In the kitchen to her sister, "Don't listen to them. You don't have to do what they say."

In the bedroom to her brother, "Don't worry. I am in charge now."

In the living room to her new father, "I love you, Daddy. You are nice. But Mommy is mean to me."

From the very beginning she used manipulation and control to define her role in our family. She didn't know any better. She didn't even understand it herself. All she knew was in order to protect herself, to protect her siblings, she needed to protect their hearts. This meant no attaching. No feeling. No loving. It meant creating barriers.

At first the barriers were small and seemingly insignificant. Whispered words. A locked door. Quietly ignoring a request.

But as the days ticked away, as we grew more comfortable with each other, the barriers grew stronger and higher. The defiance grew bolder. A screamed threat. A slammed door. Refusal to acknowledge authority.

As we prepared to leave Ethiopia, we realized we would be traveling home with more than we had bargained for. We were carrying extra baggage that would weigh us down as we transitioned our family to life in America.

The early days of most anything—a new job, a new relationship, a new venture—are usually filled with more fantasy than reality. Oh, look! Everything is shiny. Everything is beautiful. But once the shiny newness has worn off, the truth is apparent. This is not going to be as easy as we once thought. Nothing worth having ever comes easy, does it?

In 1963 Bruce Tuckman, a business leader and innovator, wrote about the four stages of group development. When creating a team—in business, in sports, and apparently in family life—these four stages are common and expected.

Forming. The initial meeting. Getting to know one another. Figuring out the dynamics of your relationship. Focus tends to be on self. People are on their best behavior.

Storming. The disagreements. The trials. Testing one another. Tensions mount as people let down their guard. Tuckman says, "Without tolerance and patience, the team will fail."

Norming. Resolving disagreements. Accepting one another. Moving on with a greater spirit of cohesiveness.

Performing. Common goals are realized. There is a high level of success. People work with one another and accept their differences.

Our family had firmly entered the storming phase. The gloves were off. It was time to do the real work of tearing down barriers, building new relationships, and loving one another through the midst of the storm. It soon became obvious that without tolerance and patience, our family would fail.

18

SHUKRIYA'S PAIN

America, 2012

Shukriya huddled in the corner of her bedroom with her arms wrapped protectively around her head. She felt the carpet against her cheek and the cold wall against her back. She pressed her hands tightly to her ears, but she could still hear the screaming. Why did her sister have to scream like that? Why did her mom always seem to be crying? Shukriya didn't like when people were fighting, but she seemed to be surrounded by it in her new home.

Coming to America, finally finding a new family, wasn't the fairy tale she had imagined it would be. In her dreams her new family was always smiling. In her dreams they did things together like shop for new clothes, sit at a dinner table so overflowing with food that there was hardly room for their elbows, play in the snow (something she had only seen in a movie one time but imagined to be as soft as the clouds). In her dreams her new family was perfect.

But real life wasn't like her dreams at all.

Shukriya heard her sister's voice cut through the closed bedroom door and seep through her fingers. "I hate you! I wish I never came to America!"

Why did she have to say that? She knew it would make her mom cry.

God, please help Hamdiya to stop saying mean things. And please help my mom to stop crying. I just want everyone to be happy. Shukriya prayed silently in the corner. She had a lot to pray about these days. She talked to God all the time, just like she did in Ethiopia. She was sure He was listening to her. He had answered her prayers before. Maybe He would do it again.

Please help my new family to be happy. Please help us to stop fighting all the time.

Shukriya didn't understand why her sister was so mad about their new family. When they lay in bed at night, Hamdiya would whisper about going back to Ethiopia. Didn't she remember how awful it had been there? Didn't she remember the empty stomachs and lonely days? It seemed all Hamdiya remembered was the good stuff: the ripening cornfields on their farm, their mom laughing in the sun, the days before everything had changed. Hamdiya promised they would go home one day, but Shukriya was confused. She felt like they *were* home.

Maybe everything wasn't perfect in America, but it felt like it could get better. If only there were more laughter and fewer tears. She knew her mom hid in her bathroom and cried a lot. She could hear her down there at night, even though she tried to be quiet about it.

Shukriya thought if she did more to help around the house, maybe that would make her mom happier. Her mom was always in the kitchen cooking or washing dishes. Tomorrow Shukriya would help her. She would wash all the dishes. She would also talk to her brothers about eating what was put before them. They were being so picky, not wanting to try new foods. Eyob was always asking for shiro and injera and pushing away his plateful of chicken and vegetables. She would explain to him that they all needed to be on their best behavior so their new family wouldn't fall apart like their old family did.

But whenever she tried to explain the way she felt to her sister, Hamdiya would just shrug her shoulders and keep talking about how she didn't care if they got sent back to Ethiopia. It almost seemed like Hamdiya was trying to make that happen. She'd better be careful. If she made their new mom and dad too mad, she would end up getting what she wanted and they would all be back at the orphanage.

The thought of going back to the orphanage made Shukriya's stomach feel sick. She decided she would do whatever she had to do to make sure that didn't happen. She would clean. She would help. She would talk to her brothers. She would never fight. If she was the perfect daughter, then her mom and dad would have to keep her.

And if she prayed hard enough, if she didn't sin too much, then God would probably listen.

God, I promise to be good. I promise to try harder. Just please help my new family to work out. Please don't let us go back to the orphanage.

19

NEVER SAY GOOD-BYE

My children have two mothers. Both of us are real mothers. Both have flesh and blood and love and pain. Both have pieces of our hearts that have been broken by good-byes. Both of us have spent too many days apart from our children.

In our home we don't classify the mothers. There is no bio mom or adoptive mom. No first mom or second mom. No tummy mom or heart mom.

Both of us are simply Mom. We need no other label.

We are cut from the same cloth. We both are women who walk through life making a lot of mistakes. We try our best. We make wrong decisions. We need extra helpings of grace. We both are living lives that turned out differently than we expected. We are two women who fiercely love their children but don't always know how to show this love in practical ways.

My children's mother is a part of our family. Her picture hangs in a place of honor in their bedrooms. Her name is a part of our vocabulary. In ways large and small, her presence fills our home.

When we were in Ethiopia, we had the honor of spending an afternoon together. Two mothers sitting in the courtyard of an orphanage, their children between them. We hired an interpreter to be better able to share our thoughts and dreams with each other. We moved into the corner office so as not to be interrupted by the crowds of orphans. We asked many questions. We knew our time together was limited, and we wanted to share memories before it was too late.

Me: Is there a special significance to the names you chose for your children? What do their names mean?

Her: What will our children do in America? Will they go to school? Will they work?

Me: What do you hope for their future?

Her: Will you bring them home to visit me?

Me: What is a special memory you have of your children? What is one thing you would want them to know about you?

Her: Will my children have cousins? Grandparents? Will their extended family be a part of their lives?

Me: What circumstances caused you to give up your children?

Her: I did not give up my children. I will never give up my children. They will always be my children. But now they are your children too. And I want to give them the chance to have a better life with you. I pray that you will now be my sister and we can love these children together.

As we sat in the office, cramped and stuffy and crowded with people and emotions, her words seemed too big for the space. They filled the air between us and pushed me into my corner. The closer I moved toward her, the more closely I was forced to examine my insecurities.

Love these children together? I wasn't even sure how to love them alone.

We filed out of the office and moved through the courtyard to the gate of the orphanage. We stood back and allowed her time to say good-bye. We watched as our children hugged their mother for what might be the last time. We took their picture together. A mother and her children. And then we walked through the opened gate together. A mother and her children.

As we were leaving, we pressed a cell phone into her hand. We decided that although we weren't sure what it might look like, we needed to love these children together with her the best we could.

Even though the details were fuzzy, we knew we

wanted to maintain our children's connection to their mother. If it was at all within our power to preserve this connection, we could do nothing less. We didn't want our children to ever look back and wonder why we kept them from their mother.

At the same time, when I was most honest with myself, I knew I also wanted to maintain some distance. How could they ever fully love and accept me as their mother if she stood between us? I would rather have her in the shadows, always a part of our relationship but slightly hidden. I was thankful for the ocean that would soon separate us. It seemed a fitting boundary to our relationship.

This cell phone would allow contact across the miles. And it would also allow separation. We could maintain our relationship within the confines of technology.

When we were home and settled in America, we explained to our children that we had given their mother a phone. We told them they could call and talk to her anytime they wanted.

At first, the calls were frequent. Conversations in a language we did not understand and were not invited into. Our children would wander the house with the phone pressed to their ear, words flowing like water. The calls lasted for an hour or more.

And in our home there were battles. Tears. Frustration. Love was being built and torn down and restructured.

As time went on, the calls happened less frequently. Conversations in a broken mix of Amharic and English. Silence filled the space between their words. Our children would sit by our sides, glancing at us for reassurance. The calls lasted only minutes.

In our home there was confusion. How were our children to love two mothers at the same time? What did that look like? How were they to reconcile their feelings of rejection with feelings of acceptance?

Eventually, our children stopped asking for phone calls. We had to initiate every time, handing them the phone and telling them it was time to talk to their mother. Conversations happened with an interpreter. Our children would sit on our lap or wrap their arms around our neck. The calls lasted only as long as we made them stay and talk.

In our home there was growth. A new family was under construction. We were building new relationships. And as with any construction, there was debris.

Our hearts are deep wells of emotion. When the water is clean, it pours out as love and acceptance and laughter and growth. However, at the bottom of every well are layers and layers of dirty sediment. Maybe there is a layer of trauma, or a layer containing a painful memory, or a layer of loss. These layers of sediment can lie, undisturbed, for hours or days at a time. But inevitably, something stirs up the layers.

That dirty mess is suddenly swimming in the water of our souls. It pours out in our behavior.

The phone calls home stirred up the water in my children's souls. The calls were reminders to guard their hearts. They were bricks my children used to shore up the wall between us and push me away in a million different ways.

And they were triggers for my own self-doubt. Could my children love me fully when there would always be another woman involved? Could I earn their love? Did I deserve their love?

They would push me away. I would doubt myself. They would doubt the validity of my love. They would test it. I would react with frustration.

One morning after a particularly tumultuous phone call home, we sat around the kitchen table and played a game. We were trying to provide stability after yet another good-bye. We wanted to ground their freshly agitated emotions in the reality of our family.

We settled around the table and took turns guessing letters for Hangman. When only a few blank spaces remained and it was my turn to guess, I guessed wrong. My daughter laughed at me as she turned to her dad.

It was his turn. He guessed the letter *A* and quickly won the game by spelling out the word *M-A-L-A-R-I-A*.

As we erased the board and prepared to start the

next round, my daughter said, "Good job, Dad. See. I told you so. Moms and daughters just aren't very close. But dads and daughters always love each other."

I excused myself from the table and went to the bathroom to cry.

"Moms and daughters just aren't very close." Maybe her words were meant as a warning to me. Maybe they were an aftereffect of the phone call home. Or maybe this was the only kind of mother-daughter relationship she understood.

How would I ever prove that it could be more? How could I cross the chasm that separated us?

I sat in the bathroom and cried about my feelings of helplessness as I looked across the width of this chasm. I cried over my internal struggle to give grace when all I wanted to do was react with anger. I cried because I was tired of accepting her rejection and responding with unconditional love. I cried because when the human heart feels rejected over and over again, it has a hard time allowing itself to love.

When the human heart feels rejected over and over again, it has a hard time allowing itself to love.

As that thought echoed in my mind, I suddenly realized that I had been dealing with her rejection for only a matter of months. She had been dealing with rejection her entire life.

I knew I needed to set the example. I needed to demonstrate the kind of love I hoped she would one day reciprocate. But our relationship was so multi-faceted. It had and continues to have nuances and innuendos and complex intricacies that I haven't yet figured out. This particular mother-daughter bond was new to me too. It did not have the weight of years of shared experiences to support it when the days were hard.

And there were plenty of hard days. Days when it all got to be too much and I was too tired to care. Days when I was short-tempered and impatient and lost sight of the endgame because the here and now was so overwhelming.

I remember one day, about a year after the adoption decree had been signed, when everything that could go wrong, did. The children were fighting, the dog had escaped and the neighbor was yelling, the doctor had called with yet another reminder that we needed to make a payment, and my daughter was raging. Two hours of screaming, slammed doors, tears, and frustration. I had finally corralled everyone for an afternoon snack. We were all sitting at the table together when my daughter started in again.

"I don't like this snack. I don't want to eat it. Why did you put more jelly on Hannah's sandwich than mine? It is because you love her more. You always treat her better than you treat me. You are so nice to her. You are mean to me. I don't like it here. I don't want to be your daughter. You don't help me. You don't take care of me. You don't—"

Something in me snapped at that moment. I stood up from my chair and slammed my open palm onto the tabletop. "Shut up! Just shut up right now!" I screamed.

The kids were shocked into silence. Wide eyes stared up at me from around the table. My daughter simply shrugged one shoulder and turned her face away. I rushed into my bedroom and collapsed into a heap on my bed. I was so upset, I was shaking. Tears streamed down my face as I quickly called my husband.

"You need to come home," I said.

He could barely understand me through the sobs.

"Wait. Calm down, honey. What's wrong?"

"I can't do this anymore. I need you to come home."

That was not the only time I felt like I couldn't do it anymore. The stress in our home was palpable.

It was hard. And it was painful. And it was messy.

But it was also necessary. Ignoring the mess is never a good solution. Clean water can cover up the sediment for only so long. The only way to be free of the mess is to stir it up and pour it out.

The journey to loving two mothers has been a difficult one for my children. There was a lot of push and pull. Barriers constructed and then torn down one heavy brick at a time. The rejection of one mother in the quest to prove allegiance to another. The eventual realization that love is strong enough to carry the weight of two mothers.

The journey to loving my children within the context of another woman's relationship has been a challenge for me. The love between my children and me was not the kind of love most women experience when they hold their newborn baby for the first time. There was not a seamless connection between their hearts and mine.

No, it took years to grow our love. Planted in the fertile soil of our family, watered with tears and prayers, grown with patience and intentional tending. My children had to give themselves permission to feel and express their love. I had to determine how to best love their mother. I had to learn how to share their hearts with another woman.

I spoke about this recently with a friend. He was adopted as an infant and did not have the opportunity to know his first mother as he was growing up. When he became a man he went searching for her.

He found her.

And he suddenly found himself living in the space between two mothers.

He told me how uncomfortable it was there. He felt hemmed in on all sides by the desire to please. He weighed his love and his relationships and always worried that one was lacking. Until one day he came to the realization that this was his story. It was not any better than other stories. It was not any worse. It simply was.

This is who he is: a child with two mothers. Once

he accepted the fact that he did not have to quantify or justify his story, he found the freedom to live it.

This is the freedom I seek. The freedom to live our family's unique story without worrying if it is better or worse or different. The freedom to love with abandon rather than calculation.

I want this freedom for my children: To love two mothers entirely, with no portioning out of affection. To embrace their story for what it is—a masterpiece written by God to include plot twists, unexpected characters, and a final chapter filled with redemption.

I want this freedom for their mother: To love her children without regret, to fully entrust their care to another woman. To believe this other woman is doing a good job raising them.

I want this freedom for myself: To know beyond a shadow of a doubt my children's love is a permanent thing. No matter where we go in life, no matter who we become, we will always be mother and child. I am theirs and they are mine and we are hers. We all are better together than we ever were apart.

My children have had to say good-bye to their mother too many times.

They said good-bye on the day she walked them into the orphanage and filled out paperwork with a trembling hand.

They said good-bye on the day we walked them

out of the orphanage and into a new life with trembling hearts.

They said good-bye every time they called home, reaching across the miles through a staticky and broken connection with trembling voices.

I never want to be the reason they have to say good-bye to her again.

20

THE BATTLE OF LETTING GO

Shortly after we returned from Africa I had a dream. It was vivid and consuming, and even now as I remember the details I can feel my heart beat faster. I startled awake, a pit deep in my stomach and my breath catching. Fear lay thick in my throat as my eyes opened to the midnight dark. I sat up quickly, feeling panicked. It was the kind of dream that felt so real, that *was* so real, I felt suspended between my subconscious and the physical world.

Needing to anchor myself back in reality, I walked up the stairs and wandered through my children's bedrooms, smoothing sticky hair from little foreheads and tucking blankets around dangling feet. I listened for their soft breathing and returned to bed only after I had reassured myself that all of my children were safe.

In my dream it was a beautiful day. My children and I were on the sandy shores of a lake, the sun shining and the sparkling water filled with laughing families. We left our towels on the beach and jumped into the water. We splashed and played with abandon, and I felt such joy.

I looked around at my children, treasuring the moment together, when I realized one was drowning. I instantly reached over and pulled them above the water, lifting their head to breathe. I treaded water, working to keep their head up, when I saw that another of my children was going under. I struggled to keep the first child afloat as I lifted another from under the waves. One by one they started to sink, and I began to panic as I worked to keep my children from drowning.

Suddenly I saw my children's hands were bound. I glanced from child to child and saw they were all bound at the wrists, unable to use their arms. I frantically pulled at knots and tried to undo the sturdy ropes tying their hands, but as I helped one child, another flailed helplessly.

My children were drowning all around me and I could not help them all. I couldn't untie all of those ropes that bound them. I wasn't strong enough to lift six drowning children out of the water and hold them up for a breath of air. I had the sickening realization that some of my children were going to sink. They would drown, and there was nothing I could do. No matter how hard I fought to help them, someone was going to die.

I didn't need a psychology degree to understand my dream. It stuck with me for days, shadowing my thoughts and coloring my emotions. Even now I can close my eyes and feel my heart quickening as I remember my helplessness as I watched my children drown.

This helplessness—the realization we were all drowning—colored many of our early days together. We had left America as a family of four. We came home as a family of eight. Doubling our family size was not the piece of cake I'd hoped it would be. (Whatever the opposite of a piece of cake is, that's what our transition felt like. Maybe burned broccoli.)

Four of our children did not speak English. Yes, they could say, "I'm thirsty," and "Why do we have to use toilet paper?" That was about the extent of our communication. But topics like fear, family, anger, loss—these were all things for which they did not yet have words. Nevertheless, in the early days, those emotions were our ever-present companions.

And when words fail, you get your message across in other ways.

One evening I walked in to find our three daughters involved in a hair-pulling, kicking, scratching, slapping, all-out girl fight. They were rolling around on the floor like crazy people. Or maybe like little girls who had each lost everything they once knew to be real.

Our three girls shared a room. This is what happens when you go from two kids to six and you don't have six bedrooms. Two of my daughters were making a statement by insisting on wearing matching pajamas every night. If my third daughter tried to put on the same pair of pajamas, they'd quickly change into something else.

My new daughters lacked the words to explain their need to create boundaries. They were building a wall of protection around their little family of four, and they were using pajamas to do it. Their matching pajamas said, "We may be living in their country, in their home, learning their language, but we don't have to belong to them. It's *us* versus *them.*"

My biological daughter heard those pajamas loud and clear. She felt excluded from her own family. Determined to be a part of the group, she changed pajamas quickly, copying her sisters' choice time after time in a frantic effort at inclusion. When the pajama-changing game failed her, she resorted to physically helping her sisters make the right choice.

For the next several weeks, I would sit in my daughters' room at bedtime and supervise their pajama choices. As my girls got ready for bed I would talk about kindness and fairness, the blessings of sisterhood, how good it feels to be included, and what it looks like to be part of a family. Although two-thirds of my girls didn't speak English, it seemed as though pieces of my message might be making it past the language barrier and into their hearts. We had more smiles and fewer tears at bedtime. We had three little girls being tucked into three little beds, each one wearing the same pajamas as her sisters.

Then one evening I left the room after everyone was safely dressed in matching pajamas, and a few moments later I heard cries of outrage. It seems two of my daughters had also donned matching underwear. They waited until I walked away to lift their nightgowns and show Hannah how she was missing out.

Oh, sure. You think it's funny. Matching underwear is a *very big deal*.

(Let me stop and say that if any of my friends ever plan a matching-underwear day and don't include me in the fun, I will be very hurt.)

Since day one we had been dealing with the dynamics of the sister triad. It was a hard adjustment for all. My Ethiopian beauties had a special, loving relationship. They had been separated for years, dreaming of the day they might be reunited. Shukriya prayed for her sister every night she was in the orphanage. She talks of lying under her blanket and crying as she petitioned God. She enlisted the help of her best friend, and they would hold hands in the dark and pray together for Shukriya to see her sister again.

When two of you get together on anything at all on earth and make a prayer of it, my Father in heaven goes into action. And when two or three of you are together because of me, you can be sure that I'll be there. (Matthew 18:19–20)

I love this passage because it demonstrates two truths. One, God was there: "And when two or three of you are together because of me, you can be sure that I'll be there," He promised. He was with my children in that orphanage. He was beside them in the dark. They were never alone. They were never forsaken. He was their father when they had none.

And two, this verse offers yet another example of answered prayer: "When two of you get together on anything at all on earth and make a prayer of it, my Father in heaven goes into action." When Shukriya and her friend clasped hands and lifted their voices together, God went into action. He moved the mountains that needed to be moved to build our family.

He brought sisters together. All three of them. Yet two of them share a common history, language, and culture. Two understand the pain of separation and the trauma of loss. Two have shared experiences that hold a special place in their hearts. So how could we build a sister relationship among all three of my girls?

I am so thankful I'm not writing a how-to book, because I don't have a magic formula. It took a lot of trial and error, patience and frustration, tears and laughter.

When I found my girls in distress over their underwear choices, what could I do but laugh? In the middle of their tears, I found myself chuckling. I thought, *I bet dollars to donuts that none of my friends are dealing with a situation quite like this right now. They probably never have to think about matching underwear. Those lucky stinkers!*

Ultimately, as with almost every issue we faced as a new family, the solution lay with the passage of time and in the Healer of all hearts. For my daughters to form a relationship, they needed to spend time together. They had to create their own set of shared experiences. They needed to be able to look back on memories that included one another.

But that's life, isn't it? One moment after another, memories being birthed in the middle of this world's mess. The bedtime struggles and the whispered apologies. The morning rush and the hurried good-byes. Homework and housework and schoolwork and days running through our fingers. Living and loving one another from dawn to dusk—and suddenly you look up and realize: *We did it.*

We weathered some storms, and we shared some laughs, and through the fires of our lives we forged our own set of memories. And maybe one day, when my girls look back on those early days together, they, too, will be able to laugh at the Great Underwear Battle.

Or maybe they'll look back and laugh at a different battle. There are so many to choose from:

- The Who Is Older: Joel or Leah? Battle
- The I Don't Need a Mother Battle
- The I Won't Get My Hair Wet Because Water Gives Me Scalp Fungus Battle
- The No Going Outside at Night Because Hyenas Will Eat You Battle
- The Why Do We Have to Change Our Underwear Every Day Battle (This one was fought valiantly by my boys, who did not understand why they should be forced to wear underwear at all but if they must wear those confounded things, then changing them once a week should be sufficient.)
- The Toilet Paper Battles of 2012–2013–2014. (This was an ongoing struggle as the little people desperately tried to overthrow the King. But He still sits on the throne. Toilet paper *will* be used. It *will* go in the toilet, *not* in the trash can. And we *never use an entire roll in the same sitting*.) This final rule was written into law after the Great Flood of 2013, which sadly spread from our bathroom, down the hallway, and through half of our living room.

And the greatest battle of all? The battle I continue to fight with myself daily? It's the *Battle of Letting Go*.

God has been teaching me how to let go. He gave me these children to teach me more about Himself. He gave me these children to show me more about His great love. And He gave me that dream as a lesson. It haunted me for weeks. I prayed about it constantly. I knew God was telling me something I needed to hear. He was reminding me I was not here to save my children. That is His job. I can never be their savior.

Those ropes that bound them? Those knots that were tied so tightly? The trauma, the loss, and the suffering from their past that was keeping my family in bondage? I could do nothing to release my children from those problems. For me, it was impossible. Only God. He is the One who can unbind. He is the One who breaks every chain. He is the Great Healer. He may use me as an agent of His healing, but He is the source.

What was God asking of me? He was asking me to love my children. He was asking me to help my children. He was asking me to let go and let Him take control.

I have found such freedom in this. Mamas, you are not responsible for the outcome. No matter how your children came to you, through birth or through adoption, those children belong to God. They are His. We are simply the caretakers of His treasures. We are not responsible for the finished product. He is. He has all the accountability, and He gets all the glory for the people they will become. Who our children grow up to be, the choices they make, the lives they lead—those are not our burdens to carry.

Yes, we have an obligation when we take on the job of mother. We are promising to try our very best. Yes, we have guidelines we should follow as we raise our children. But at the end of the day, I am responsible for only *my* actions and *my* heart.

Even though I know this now, although God reminds me of this time and again, it tends to become a sort of tug-of-war, with God gently pulling on His end and me alternating between holding on tight and again letting go.

Loving my children is an ongoing exercise in learning to let go: Letting go of my expectations. Letting go of my control. Letting go of everything I thought I had planned for my life. In that struggle of give-and-take, push-and-pull, I have found joy.

21

THE SPACE BETWEEN US

In the world of quantum physics, it's understood that objects never actually touch. Two objects can move toward each other and appear to press up against each other. To the casual observer it seems they're touching. But way down deep on the atomic level, there will always be a space between them. The Pauli exclusion principle states that electrons are always working to push away from one another.

I fear this principle also applies to me.

I think of the spaces that fill our lives. The space between asked and answered questions when we pause to frame a response. The space between women that can be filled with envy or judgment. The space between our words that's often filled with a secondary meaning. The heavy space between the angry voices in an argument. The space that keeps expanding the longer it takes to find or offer forgiveness.

I think of my husband and how the space between his heart and mine has all but disappeared in the years of our marriage. Our hearts were close when we first said our vows, but when you walk through the fires of life with someone, the heat can't help but shrink-wrap the space between you. I think of my now-teenage son and how the space between us has grown wider as he tests his independence and finds his autonomy.

Every relationship has a space built into it, whether intentional or not. In some relationships the space is so small, it's barely discernible. In others, more space is needed to protect ourselves.

Hear me when I say that love and space are two different things, though they are similar ingredients in the family recipe. In a family, you want as much love as you can get. The more love you add to the mix, the less room is left for the spaces between you. Yet sometimes love and space get all mixed together and one can feel like the other.

I love all of my children. And the longer I know them, the more I find to love about them. The sound of Levi Eyob's laughter—loud and contagious. The warmth of Hannah as she crawls into my bed every morning for a hug to start her day. The fierce determination with which Micah Eba learns and loves and lives. The quiet way Naomi Shukriya moves through life—never demanding attention, always noticing others, and always the first to offer help. The beautiful song that lives inside

Leah Hamdiya—my dancer, my singer, my performer. She was made to shine. The brilliant mind and fiercely loyal heart Joel exhibits as he moves into his teen years.

I love all these things about them and so much more. But the depth of my love cannot erase all the space between us. No matter how hard I try to get close to them, something is always working to push me away. My own personal Pauli exclusion principle. (I've never liked physics very much.)

The space between me and my adopted children has been decreasing since the day I first learned of their existence. Every bit of our togetherness has been intentional. We inch our way toward one another—our progress halting, sometimes stalling, sometimes regressing, never easy. We had a greater distance to travel than most. My goodness, we began half a world apart!

Slowly and deliberately we have moved toward one another. Paperwork and prayers. Airplane rides and adoption decrees. Each of these narrowed the space. Then one day we found ourselves pressed against one another—living in the same home, belonging to the same family, spending our days all entangled with each other. Yet there was still a space between us that an outside observer might never notice. Most of the time I can even fool myself into believing the space does not continue to exist.

Until I can no longer ignore it.

When we walk down the street together, people don't automatically assume we are a family. When we are running errands I often get the question "Are you on a field trip?" or sometimes "Do you do foster care?" I know people aren't asking out of malice. But my children hear these questions, which can create a space.

My children have a different skin color than I have. Their voices are accented. They have to be careful when taking medications with codeine because Ethiopians can have allergic reactions to this drug. They put coconut oil in their hair. The winter months are especially hard on their skin, and they have to use extra moisturizer to prevent ashiness and cracking. None of these attributes are better or worse than any other, but they are different from mine. These differences can create a space.

Then there was the family tree project in third grade. The request for a baby picture for the fifth-grade Student of the Week poster. The eighth-grade graduation slideshow—please send in a picture from when they were in kindergarten. Studying genetics in sixth grade and filling in the blanks: *Did you get your eye color from your mom or your dad? Which recessive trait might you have gotten from your parents?* Blank space. Blank space. More created space.

Vast portions of my children's stories I may never know. Years and years of experiences may never be remembered or shared—memories that are their very own to hold tight. Those unshared memories create a space.

There is trauma in my children's past. There is fear and hurt and anger. Those emotions create a space.

There is another family. Another mother. Another father. Loved and lost. But forever a part of them. A part of us. A part of the space.

Imagine with me for a moment: You wake up tomorrow and turn over to find an empty pillow beside you. You get up and look for your spouse, your children. Where are they? Where could they have gone? Surely they would not leave you. Your entire family could not simply disappear. You run from room to room, frantically searching the empty beds. You throw open closet doors, look in the dark corners, your heart pounding. You cry out, screaming their names over and over. Only silence. No one is there. Everyone you love is gone. They have been ripped from your life. Torn away. You are grief-stricken, panicked, inconsolable. You sink to the floor, unable to walk, talk, think.

As you lie in the middle of your grief, a group of strangers suddenly appears in your home. They open the door and walk inside as if they belong, smiles on their faces, arms open wide, voices loud with excitement. They begin sleeping in those empty beds and sitting at your kitchen table. They tell you they'll be your replacement family—and they are so excited to share your life.

Wait a minute. Why are you crying? You should be happy. Sure, your first family is missing, but now we are here! Come on, give us a hug and a kiss. We are going to live the rest of our lives together.

But you don't want a replacement family. You want your old life back—the life filled with everything and everyone you've ever loved.

Can you understand why my children were having a hard time transitioning to America? To our family? To their new home? They didn't have room in their hearts for a new family. Their hearts were still wounded and bleeding, filled with the memories of all they had lost. It felt better, it felt safer, for them to reserve some space between us. So they set to work to create more space. With:

- Tantrums
- Rages
- Icy silences
- Meltdowns

Some of the first English words they learned were "I wish I could kill myself."

How do you tell the difference between trauma-induced exclamations and actual suicidal tendencies? This was a question we'd never had to consider. We entered uncharted territory with statements and actions that included the following:

- "You are not my family. You don't really love me. I want to go back to Ethiopia." Common. Expected. Normal, if you will. The usual pitfalls and roadblocks on the adoption journey.
- "I hate myself. I want to die." That was cause for concern, an obstacle not clearly marked on our map.
- Tattooing the word *bad* on a wrist. This act of labeling oneself as damaged goods was evidence we had strayed wildly off course. We needed to seek help fast.

We now refer to this time in our life as "Hell Week." But that season was more serious than the tongue-in-cheek name suggests. And it lasted far longer than a week.

During those early months, our children quickly grasped the basics of the English language. Complete immersion will do that. Their vocabulary grew daily. And as they finally found the words they'd been seeking, the details of their lives began to emerge.

Their stories were filled with suffering and laced with horror. We heard things you never want to hear from the mouths of your babies. We were completely unprepared to deal with this level of pain. We needed help. We needed some professional pain management.

We enlisted the help of a counselor.

I'll freely tell anyone, if you need a counselor, then by all means go to see a counselor! Counselors, therapists, psychiatrists: Hallelujah! These professions are here to help us navigate life's hard road. I wish everyone who needed these services had access to them. So many of us are struggling to make it from day to day. If it is pride holding you back—get over it. Every person in our family has been in counseling. Every single one. And we all are better for it. Counseling is for those who are strong enough to admit they need a little help navigating this broken world.

Counseling is expensive but worth every penny. If someone says they can't afford it, I suggest they do a little research. Maybe there are some free counseling services nearby. Call some churches. Many pastors and lay pastors offer free counseling.

When we entered our own special Hell Week and realized we were in over our heads, we researched counseling options. Our insurance paid for only a handful of sessions. Barely enough to make a dent in the misery. Yet we were living in a state of triage. Slapping Band-Aids on severed limbs, bleeding out faster than we could apply tourniquets.

Oh yes, God was there. He was in the midst of all the hurt. He saw our wounds, and He held our tears in His hands. He is the Great Physician. He never left our sides. But we also needed someone with skin on. Someone with whom our children could share the scariest, darkest, messiest parts of their lives. Someone who had the patience and wisdom to respond appropriately. Someone who had strategies to help us all deal with the pain.

God sent us Miss Colleen.

Miss Colleen had been a children's counselor for more than thirty years. She had seen it all, heard it all, and prayed over it all. Miss Colleen had the strategies we needed to make it through Hell Week, no matter how long it might last.

And she was not going to charge us a dime.

The first time we sat in front of her, she told us she would not accept any payment from our family. Ever. She said she took God at His word in James 1:27, where He says the church is called to minister to orphans and widows.

She was the church to us.

Miss Colleen ministered to the orphans and widows, to the sons and daughters, to every member of our family for as long as we needed. We met with her almost every week—for three years. We shared all of our pains and fears. We cried into her throw pillows. We figuratively bled all over her beautiful office. We opened our wounds so they could heal. My children. Myself. My husband. My mother. Singly and in pairs. Brothers and sisters. Together. Husband and wife. Together. Mother and daughter. Together. Miss Colleen gave us the tools to bridge the spaces between us.

We used those tools again and again. We worked and we prayed and we chipped away at the hard spaces in our family.

With the help of Miss Colleen, with the help of God, those spaces started to disappear. Maybe not entirely. But they were getting smaller and smaller.

It was in Miss Colleen's office where my oldest daughter took a step toward me, lessening the space between us. She laid her head in my lap and admitted she was afraid of losing me. The fear was what had been driving her to create space with her words and her actions.

This particular counseling session came on the heels of weeks of storms in our home. We had been making progress as a family, inching our way toward one another, and yet something had stirred the sediment in the water.

Scott and I had decided to go away together. We had been a family for one and a half years. One and a half years of intentional togetherness with our children. Our marriage needed some attention, and so we arranged to go on a minivacation, just the two of us.

When we told the children, there was no immediate reaction. The shock waves were under the surface, though, gaining momentum and strength, until they could be contained no longer and erupted into our daily lives.

Anger. Manipulation. Regression. We had taken

so many steps forward, and now we were taking multiple steps back.

I stood outside my spin class one day, sweaty and spent. I was exhausted both physically and emotionally. When a friend stopped to ask how I was doing, the tears came.

"I am tired of all of it. Maybe we shouldn't go on vacation. It is getting too hard to deal with the anger. It might be more trouble than it's worth."

My words echoed in my mind as we drove to the counselor's office that afternoon. My daughter sat hunched in her seat, body turned away from me, staring out the window. She was doing her best to pretend I wasn't in the car with her. I was left alone with my tumultuous thoughts.

We both cried in Miss Colleen's office that day, my daughter's tears mirroring my own. We sat in our separate chairs and allowed our words to create a barrier between us. Until Miss Colleen said something we both needed to hear.

"I don't think either of you are angry at the other. I think you are scared."

These words propelled my daughter out of her chair. She crossed the distance between us, dropped onto the floor, and laid her head in my lap.

"I don't want you to leave, Mom. I don't like it when people leave me. What if you never come back?"

Her words cracked the door open to both her

heart and mine. They gave voice to our fears: the fear of losing each other, the fear of losing ourselves. Her words chipped away at the space between us.

God was doing what is physically impossible. He wrote the laws of physics, and He can suspend them when He chooses. His love is the glue that bonds our family. The spaces between us are shrinking. I have to squint into the bright light of our Father's love to see those spaces anymore.

22

PERSPECTIVE

In December, only five months after bringing our children home, we celebrated my daughter's tenth birthday. I was battle-worn and weary, but determined to prove to my oldest daughter how special she was. I wanted to make up for all the missed birthdays in her past. I decorated and I baked and I wrapped her present with a big bow on top. I invited our extended family to join in the festivities.

The day of her birthday was cloudy and cold. Inside our home, however, it was bright and cheery. I placed her cake on the kitchen table as I lit the candles. Our family gathered around. For the very first time in her life, Leah blew out her birthday candles surrounded by people who loved her. We sang "Happy Birthday" as we took her picture.

My daughter hated it. She hated every single thing about it. She did not want to celebrate her tenth birthday because she felt it was a lie. It wasn't her actual birthday. The courts in Ethiopia had assigned a birth date to each of my children. No one knows the day and time they were born. Except God. He formed each one of them and numbered their days.

You know me inside and out, you know every bone in my body; you know exactly how I was made, bit by bit, how I was sculpted from nothing into something. Like an open book, you watched me grow from conception to birth; all the stages of my life were spread out before you, the days of my life all prepared before I'd even lived one day. (Psalm 139:13–16)

But on this side of heaven, we had to guess at their ages. My daughter wasn't turning ten, and we all knew it to be true. She was probably already eleven. And December 6 was most certainly not the day she was born. But this will now be her birthday forever. It is the date chosen to celebrate her life, regardless of the number on top of the cake.

She made her birthday miserable. For herself and for everyone who loved her. My heart broke watching her sabotage all the joy around her. It was as if she didn't believe she deserved anything good so she twisted it into something bad with the poison of her words and her actions.

Besides the fact that it wasn't her *real* birthday, the celebration served to remind her of the fact that she was not the oldest. Ever since joining our family, she had had to relinquish the title of Oldest Child to Joel. This was not something easily done.

Leah basically raised her three younger siblings. Her mother was absent for long periods of time in order to earn money for their family to survive. Leah was left in charge. She figured out how to strap her baby brother onto her back and carry him with her while she tended the fire. How to entertain her sister with nothing more than corn husks and twigs. How to divide their single meal of the day into tiny portions and spread them out as evenly as possible between the hours and the hungry stomachs. Leah was forced to become a leader, and it was not a role she planned to surrender.

My son, on the other hand, was comfortable as the firstborn. He was used to being the top dog among our children. He relished his role as king and was not willing to abdicate his throne.

These two were like oil and water. We tried to mix them together to create one family, but they would have none of it. Neither one was about to kowtow to the other. There were arguments and tears and frustration for all of us.

Our counselor was a godsend. She provided us with the tools we were so desperately searching for. Miss Colleen validated our feelings—all our feelings. No one person's feelings took precedence over any other's. Our feelings were legitimate and deserved;

the pitfalls were found in how we allowed those feelings to influence our behaviors.

She helped me to realize I was overcompensating. I was trying so hard to prove my love for my daughter that I often ignored what she really needed. She did not need a big birthday party with all the trimmings and excitement. She needed me to come alongside her as she searched for herself.

Leah had lost everything she once thought to be true about who she was. She lost her country. Her language. Her food. Her family. Even her name. She was adrift in this new life, and she was grasping at any token of her identity that might help her find her way. If one of those tokens was her status as oldest child, that was a position I could validate.

Miss Colleen helped my son to realize there was room for two at the top of the pyramid. He was no less my firstborn than he had been before we doubled our family. He was willing to give a little, take a little, and learn how to collaborate on the job of oldest child.

Our counselor taught my daughter some techniques for coping with her feelings. She put together a feelings bag. Inside was a stress ball, a journal, bubbles, a pack of gum. Whenever my daughter's feelings overwhelmed her, when she felt she could no longer control her behavior, she was to retrieve her feelings bag and find some quiet space to be alone.

Counseling helped Leah to realize that the number on a birth certificate did not need to define her. We all acknowledged that number to be false. And yet we were stuck with it. So we made the best of it. We decided that both of our oldest children needed to be afforded the special privileges and the unique responsibilities that came along with their job title.

The first step was rearranging bedrooms. This was not an easy task for a family of eight who lived in a home with only four bedrooms. We had to build an extra room in the garage. We moved my son out there, into his own "man cave." Then we gave Leah her own space, the corner room with windows looking out over the treetops.

Every night we tuck our four littles into bed and say their prayers with them. We turn out the lights and close the bedroom doors. We allow our two oldest children to stay up a little later. They can choose a quiet activity—reading, finishing homework, listening to music. This "late night" time is something they both enjoy as a perk of being the oldest.

My oldest children had to work hard on their relationship. It was not something that improved overnight. And there is still work to be done. For all of us. We are a work in progress.

Too often the only voice heard in the adoption community is that of the adoptive parent. Our voice is the loudest. Our position the most dominant. And yet we are only one small piece of the puzzle. The adopted child, the bio parents, the siblings already in the home—their voices need to be heard. Their positions need to be elevated. As our counselor taught us, no one person's feelings take precedence over any other's. In the hope of adding texture and flavor to the adoption conversation, I asked my son Joel to share how adoption changed his life:

Leah and I have always had an especially complicated relationship. As the oldest of my adopted siblings, she was in many ways the most affected by her experiences in Ethiopia. Leah is very kind and loving, but she had a hard past and can sometimes be hard to connect with.

One of the hardest things about adjusting to our family for Leah was giving up authority over her siblings. In Ethiopia they were constantly on their own, just the four of them. They moved from family to family, from orphanage to orphanage. Thus, Leah took charge, caring for and providing for her siblings. They developed a special bond. Leah became more than their sister, she became their leader.

Even though Leah and I have had more than our fair share of problems, I know that she loves me. We fight often, but we always get over our dispute eventually. Leah is a good and kind person and I desire to have a close relationship with her. Many of our fights and issues are just as much my fault as hers. Slowly, with lots of prayer, our relationship is getting better. Overall our relationship is doing OK, but I would still like to be closer to her.

The adjustment to our family for the rest of my siblings was not quite as hard as Leah's, in my opinion. However, they all still faced their own challenges. My other adopted sister, Naomi, is now nearly inseparable from my biological sister, Hannah. But the beginning of their relationship did not go so well. When they first met they fought all of the time and didn't seem to like each other very much. Neither of them was in the wrong, they just could not get along with each other. Their relationship healed with time, though, and they are now the best of friends.

Before other people adopt, I would want them to know why they are doing it. Adopting children as a way to do a good deed isn't enough, you need to truly want to expand your family. I would also want them to be wary of taking advice. We prepared a lot before we adopted, and it was good that we did, but no two adopted children are the same. I think sometimes prior knowledge of problems that you might face can influence how you see your adopted family members. One more thing to remember is to not neglect your biological family members when you adopt. Even though adopted family members can need extra help, don't forget to spend time with your biological siblings and children.

In some ways my life is harder because we adopted,

*but it isn't worse. I have to deal with constant noise,
I honestly get less attention from my parents, and I
don't get a lot of personal space, but adoption made
my life better. I always have someone to talk to or
hang out with, and my siblings have added so much
to my life.*

*I have never wished that we didn't adopt. I some-
times feel like my siblings drive me crazy, but I am
still glad we adopted. This isn't because I feel like we
did a good deed, that isn't how I see it. We adopted
to expand our family, and it let a lot more joy into
our lives. I truly believe that I would be less happy
if we hadn't adopted. I don't know what my family
would be like if we hadn't adopted. It is just a part of
us now. It is just who I am.*

My son said it perfectly: Adoption is a part of us
now. It is just who we are.

23

RELEARNING HOW TO PARENT

When my daughter Hannah was about six years old, she decided to stop getting haircuts. She had grand aspirations of becoming a Disney Princess and thought the first step toward realizing her dreams was to have long, flowing locks. I indulged her desires until her hair became unmanageable. When our morning routine had devolved into tears and frustration as I yanked the brush through the tangled knots, I pulled the plug on her princess dreams and took her to the hair salon.

When my son Micah had been home about a year, he also decided to stop getting haircuts. He told me he wanted to see how long he could grow his curls. He told me he wanted an Afro. He told me he was scared of the barber. He told me half-truths and lies.

As time went on, I began campaigning for a haircut. His curls were long and messy and he didn't take the time to run coconut oil from roots to tips. His hair was getting dry at the ends and I was embarrassed by the mess on top of his head. I worried if we were out in public and a black woman saw us together, she would be silently condemning me for not doing right by my child's heritage.

One evening I sat on the corner of Micah's bed while I tucked the covers around him. I absently ran my fingers through his thick curls while I said his prayers.

When I finished, I leaned over to kiss him good night.

"Hey, Mom," said Micah, "I like it when you do that."

"Do what, buddy?"

"I like it when you run your fingers through my hair. You do it almost every night when you tuck me in."

"Oh, good! I'm glad you like it."

"I like it so much that I don't want to get my hair cut. I think if I cut my curls too short, then you might not run your fingers through my hair anymore."

All of his previously stated reasons for growing out his hair were excuses. The truth was, he was trying to protect that small connection we shared every night at bedtime.

I did end up taking him in for a haircut, but I continued the nightly tradition, making a point to run my fingers through his hair as I say his prayers.

From the moment I met my daughter Leah, she would not get her hair wet. She did not want to wash it in the shower. She wore a bathing cap if we went in the pool. She would not even allow me to use a spray bottle when styling her hair in the morning. She insisted on yanking a brush through her dry curls. No matter how I tried to convince her to allow me to help her, she preferred to comb and style her hair without my assistance.

I pleaded.

I cajoled.

I argued.

I admitted defeat.

I had to choose my battles, and I wasn't going to allow her hairstyle to become another foothold for anger in our new relationship.

After several months, I took her to a hairstylist. I called the salon ahead of time and explained my predicament. I asked if they would be willing to discuss hair care with my daughter while they trimmed her dead ends. I thought she might be willing to listen to a professional who was not her mother.

It worked. The hairstylist explained how to properly care for my daughter's beautiful curls and my daughter listened! Then she asked, "But won't I get fungus if I get my hair wet?"

"Fungus? What do you mean?"

"In Ethiopia lots of people had fungus in their

hair. My mom told me not to use the water because I might get fungus too."

Suddenly I understood. She was following her mother's instructions. She was doing her best to obey, and she didn't understand that while the water her mother was referring to most likely carried fungus, the water here in America was clean and safe.

Three children. Three situations. Three origins of behavior.

Hannah: princess dreams.

Micah: desire for connection.

Leah: fears from her past.

These are just a few examples, rather benign ones at that, of how my children's behavior stemmed from unfamiliar places. I could give you other examples. I could tell you about the screaming tantrums, the silent treatments, the hurled insults. I could talk about the nightly rituals: lying in their beds for hours upon hours trying to teach them how to fall asleep, waking in the middle of the night, nightmares involving fire and hyenas and machetes, turning lights on to mimic the brightness of day. The dark of the night was where their deepest fears lived. I could go on and on about the tangled mess of behaviors and emotions we were dealing with.

There were hundreds of new behaviors to figure out. I had to ask myself, Why *is my child acting this way? Where is this behavior coming from?* What *is the best way for me to address this?*

I asked myself these questions time and again. And then I questioned my own behavior. Did I react appropriately? Did I cause more harm than good? Why in the world did God ever think I was the right mother for these children? I was constantly questioning. Them. Me. God. Everything I once thought I knew had proved to be inadequate. When I became a mom to six children, I had to relearn how to parent.

When I had two children, I parented from the gut.

When I had six children, I had to learn how to parent from the mind.

When I had two children, I trusted my heart's instinct.

When I had six children, I had to check my feelings at the door.

When I had two children, I could look into their past and understand the origin of their fears.

When I had six children, I had to look past the behavior to the root cause of the issue.

I was quickly educated in the ways of parenting children from hard places. There was a very steep learning curve. Every day I tried new tactics. Every day I failed at some and excelled at others. Every day I searched for the best ways to connect while correcting. Applying this principle to six children, a dozen different behaviors, hundreds of hours of drama, and thousands of tears was exhausting.

Relearning how to parent was exhausting. I had to figure out how to be a soft place for my children to land but also have a hard shell that protected my heart from my children's behavior. I struggled to find the right balance. I felt like I was getting it wrong more than I was getting it right.

When I felt that I couldn't mother for one minute longer, when my brain and my heart were on overload and I knew I was at my breaking point, I would call Bethany. Bethany was my friend, babysitter, nanny, and God's gift to me in our time of need. She had been there with us from the beginning, willing to step into the trauma and get dirty. She provided us with respite, taking our place for a few hours at a time: holding children while they cried, sitting outside bedroom doors at bedtime to provide a sense of safety, willing to love our family both because of and despite the extra grace we required. She was there to pick up my slack when I was completely exhausted.

During those days of exhaustion, many people would say to me, "Oh, all kids do that. All kids act that way. All kids have that kind of behavior." I know they were saying this to try to encourage me, but it had the opposite effect. It made me feel isolated, as if no one really understood what I was dealing with.

And they didn't. They didn't understand. How could they? It wouldn't be fair of me to expect them to understand.

The late Dr. Karyn Purvis, former director of Texas Christian University's Institute of Child Development, developed research-based strategies for parenting children from hard places. She cowrote *The Connected Child: Bring Hope and Healing to Your Adoptive Family*, one of the first resources I recommend to any of my friends who are considering adoption. In the video series 10 Questions Adoptive Parents Ask, this is what she had to say about relearning how to parent:

The parent will say, "Well, do you think this is an adoption issue or do you think that this is a six-year-old boy issue?" And I'll say yes. It's really both. All children have similar behaviors. When you look at frequency, intensity, and duration, does it happen more often, does it last longer, and does it happen in ways that are more intense; those will give you some indicators of how proactive you need to be in seeking help. But you have to remember that although all children are going to, for example, break their toys sometimes, all children are going to color in the book you didn't want colored in, all children are going to argue with a sibling, all children are going to occasionally tease another child, how we recognize the behavior and how we address the behavior may be modified dramatically by the child's history. So if my child has been with me from conception forward, I was able to protect them in utero and postnatally, and now he's fighting with his brother, he can still feel shamed if I come on harshly. But if I have a child that I didn't protect and he's in that same situation, the capacity for deterioration in his behavior based on my response is far more intense. Because now I've got a child who's far more fragile in how he feels about himself, how he feels about those who would protect him, how he feels about his world. So is it about adoption? Yes. Is it about regular development? Yes. Does it matter? In some ways. Do I have to be more compassionate and more insightful? Absolutely yes. If your child is from a hard place. Absolutely yes. Be aware many tools that are used with children who do not have histories of maltreatment or harm are going to be dramatically counterproductive for our children. So if you're addressing it as a normal developmental behavior or an adoption issue, always remember where your child has come from.

When I had two children, I was a great mom.

When I had six children, I was the World's Okayest Mom.

I started losing children. Some would say I also started losing my mind.

The first time it happened, it wasn't so much that I lost a child, but rather that I lost track of time.

We had been home for about six months and I was constantly counting heads. The children's English was still spotty, their attachment to me still new, and the possibility of a child wandering off seemed very real.

As we left the gymnastics studio one day, I counted six heads around me and started the trek toward the car. My daughter suddenly had to pee. Right then. It was urgent. I walked the child to the single-stall bathroom and reached inside to flip the light switch.

"Go to the bathroom, honey. I will take everyone to the car and buckle them in. See the car right there?" I said as I pointed through the floor-to-ceiling windows lining the front of the building. "I will wait for you right there. You can see me from here."

My daughter nodded and I turned the lock on the door before closing her in.

I herded the other five children toward the door. We got sidetracked by the drinking fountain, the sparkly leotards my daughter insisted were necessary in order to become a successful gymnast, and another mom who stopped to ask about the schedule for the following week. Finally exiting the building, I loaded everyone into the van, handed out snacks, turned on the movie, double-checked seat belts, answered a phone call from my husband, and finally noticed that my daughter was taking an extraordinarily long time in the bathroom.

"Wait right here, kids. I am going to check on Naomi," I said as I hurried back inside the building.

As I entered the lobby, I heard muffled sobbing from behind the bathroom door.

"Honey! Naomi! What's wrong?" I called through the closed door.

"Mooooooooooom!" wailed Naomi from inside. "Why you leave me?"

"Baby! What is wrong?"

"You leave me. I think you gone forever!"

"I didn't leave you, honey. Open the door!"

"I can't," she said through her sobs.

"What do you mean? Open the door," I said calmly.

"I can't. No open."

"Honey, it is locked. You have to unlock it first, then turn the handle,"

"I no know how." Naomi's sobs grew louder as I realized my mistake.

I had turned the lock and closed the door without realizing she had never seen a locking mechanism like this before. She had absolutely no idea how it worked or what to do to get herself out of the bathroom.

I pressed myself up against the door and gave my best step-by-step instructions. My little English-language learner was on the other side, trying her best to escape from the bathroom prison. I spoke loudly and slowly. She cried and cried. The people in the lobby watched and marveled.

When she finally calmed down enough to hear

me, she unlocked the door and emerged from the bathroom. Shaky and spent, she pointed her finger at me and said loudly, "You say you no leave me!" and then marched out to the car, her head held high.

I followed her to the car and wrapped my arms around her. I apologized for scaring her and told her I had not left her. I would never leave her. I looked at my children, wide-eyed in the back of our van, and promised them, "I will never leave you. I am here forever."

Then I left my son at McDonald's.

I'd like to give my husband 51 percent of the credit for this mishap. After all, he was the one who walked out of the men's room and left our son inside.

We had the brilliant idea of taking ten children to an amusement park for the day. This was our first mistake.

The amusement park is a solid three-hour drive from our house. We got up at dawn and loaded our van with ten children, seven hundred water bottles, and enough snacks to survive the end times. Three hours down, eight hours at the park, and three hours home. What could go wrong?

The children had a marvelous time. The parents almost died of exhaustion. We were less than an hour from home, mere minutes from completing the trek with a spotless safety track record, when we made the fateful stop. Mommy needed some caffeine.

I unloaded my husband and the ten children at

McDonald's to use the restroom. I ran through the Starbucks next door. I pulled back into the McDonald's parking lot and rolled open the sliding door. In rushed the children. My husband climbed into the passenger seat. Locked and loaded, we headed back down the open road.

Until a child (a very observant child I might add) called from the backseat, "Where's Levi?"

I stopped my twelve-passenger van so fast I gave half of the children whiplash. I ordered my husband out of the car right there in the middle of the road. "What were you thinking? You left Levi in the bathroom? RUN! Run back now!"

I had to circle the block and come back around to McDonald's. I pulled in from one side of the parking lot just as my husband came hustling in from the other side. We met in the middle and what did we see? Levi was standing inside McDonald's, nose pressed against the glass door, fingers splayed wide, palms flat, eyes teary.

"I saw you leave me. I saw you driving away and I thought, 'I am going to live at McDonald's forever now. I will have to eat french fries until I die,'" said our overly dramatic seven-year-old.

His keenly developed dramatic tendencies are a result of his past.

In my newly defined role as mother, I had to continually remember where my children came from. I didn't adopt only the children, I adopted their history too. It was a part of them and now it was a part of our family.

So in the evening light as our daughter lay crying in the corner and said, "I just want to go back to Ethiopia," I tried to quiet my heart and lead with my mind. Her history filled the space between her words. It colored their meaning. It framed my response. *What should I say? What does she need from me right now?*

Our goal was to remain as positive as possible about our children's history. We didn't want to speak negatively about their homeland, their family, or their memories. And yet the reality of their past wasn't always pretty.

"We will go back someday and visit, but it wasn't a good situation for you there, honey," I said in what I thought was a loving and supportive tone.

I chose the wrong thing to say.

She flew out of the bedroom, ran down the hallway, and slammed her door.

My husband and I sat on the carpet outside her bedroom and listened to her cry. We leaned our foreheads against the door and allowed her space to grieve. We let her know we were nearby, ready but willing to wait.

Through the door we said, "We are so thankful to your mom and dad."

"They gave us you."

"You are a gift."

"We are sorry if we hurt your feelings. We never want to say anything bad about your parents because they gave us their most precious possession—their children."

And when our daughter finally emerged, she looked us in the eye and said, "You don't love me. You don't really want me as your daughter. If you did, you would have said you don't want me to go back to Ethiopia."

Her earlier words had carried a hidden message. When she said, "I just want to go back to Ethiopia," what she really meant was "Do you want to send me back to Ethiopia? Or do you love me enough to want me to stay here with you?"

I have never been very fluent at reading between the lines. I didn't always find the underground meaning in my children's words or actions.

I didn't always have the right response.

I didn't always use the right tone of voice.

I didn't always choose connection over correction.

But I did my best.

And it turns out that my best was all God wanted from me.

I was the okayest kind of mom, and that was enough.

24

WHISPERS OF LOVE

How many times a day do you tell your children that you love them? How often do you hear them say the same? I used to take those words for granted. Adoption taught me that hearing "I love you" is a privilege, not a right. This privilege, these beautiful words, came so easily from the mouths of our biological children. We were earning their love from the first moments of their existence. They easily fell into trusting the validity of our love. It has not been as easy with our adopted children.

Years ago, before we had ever seen our adopted children's faces or heard their names, we were praying for them. We were loving them. Oh, that love did not have the same depth or strength as the love that now flows from our souls, but we loved them from afar. God had planted the seeds of an everlasting love in our hearts. He was starting the process of building a family.

Our children, however, were on the other side of the world, and they were in the process of losing a family. They were not thinking of us or praying for us or hoping for us. They were not loving us. In fact, they might have even been blaming us. My children came to me with years of life experience I will never fully know about. Those missing years will never be recovered. Missing years and a missing country. A forgotten language. A lost father and a lost mother. That is a lot to bring into a relationship.

They did not come to us with open arms and hearts filled with love. They came to us with scars and pain. We had to earn their love. And we had to teach them how to love. From the very beginning, from the very first time that we wrapped our arms around our children, we were teaching them love.

This . . . this is what love feels like, we were showing with our arms.

This . . . this is what love looks like, we were demonstrating with our actions.

This . . . this is what love sounds like, we were communicating every time we responded to bitterness with kindness.

It was a foreign idea to our children. In the beginning they sometimes allowed the love, sometimes pushed it away, but never initiated. We would tuck our boys in every night, and I would physically place their little arms around my neck and teach them how to hug. I would say, "I love you so much, boys.

Now it's your turn. You say, 'I love you, Mommy.'"
There were times they would parrot the words back.
But mostly there was silence in the face of this un-
known feeling.

I would kiss my girls on the cheek, run my finger-
tips over their foreheads, and whisper, "I love you"
in their ears... and they would lie still in their beds
wondering at the strangeness of it all.

My children believed love to be a fragile thing,
an emotion easily broken and discarded. My job was
to provide them with a new definition of love. The
problem was that I was having to redefine it for myself. The kind of love I had always believed in was
being tested.

Up until this point in my life, love had come
fairly easily to me. Yes, I had encountered the usual
pitfalls: high school frenemies, teenage romances
gone south, the newlywed arguments that inevitably
follow the honeymoon. These arguments were cen-
tered around the Big Three: sex, money, and in-
laws. My husband's family is very private. They
tend to be quiet and calm and well-behaved. They
like to keep most of their opinions to themselves
and speak in well-modulated voices. My family is
exactly the same, except the opposite. Nothing is
off-limits. Boundaries? What are those? Everything
is about Big Feelings and Big Emotions, and it is
better if these things are discussed in loud, overlap-
ping voices.

In the early days of our marriage we had to figure out how to argue. We came to the table with vastly different strategies, and it took many failed attempts for us to learn to fight fair. But as in every long-term relationship, we had settled into a rhythm that worked well for us. Our marriage was a place of safety and security for me.

Until we adopted four children from Ethiopia and I entered the storming phase in every relationship I held dear.

Adoption affects not only children. It affects parents, extended family, friends. It affects the church, the support network, the teachers. Adoption casts a wide net. Those who are closest to you are going to be pulled in whether they like it or not.

Most people caught in the net of our adoption did not sign up for the journey. They were innocent bystanders. It was not their choice to so drastically change their lives. I remember a conversation I had with my mother shortly after we came home. We were in the middle of the worst of the drama. I was in tears about the latest battle fought in our home. And she told me, "Natalie, you never asked me if you should adopt. You didn't ask my opinion or advice. It wasn't a conversation between us. It was an announcement. You just sat me down and told me you were going to do it."

I know the conversation my mother was referring to. I had approached it with excitement. Scott and I had been talking about adoption for months at that point and had finally made the decision to move forward. I invited my mom over for dinner and made what I considered to be a "We're pregnant!" kind of announcement.

I never realized other people might not view it the same way.

My mother never signed up for this journey, but now she was taking it with me. Adoption affected our relationship. We had to go through our own storm.

My peaceful life was filled with more storms than I had ever encountered before. My safe and secure marriage was suddenly rocky. My husband and I had to work through a lot of pain before we found our healing. But the pain was necessary. We had to dig through a lot of junk to find the treasure we had been given. Isn't this what God wants for us? He wants to help us deal with our junk so we can live in the fullness of the treasures He has given us.

Some of the pain was child-inflicted: pitting one parent against the other, manipulating because it was safer than feeling, demanding the time and energy we would have normally reserved for our spouse.

Some of the pain was self-inflicted: doubting myself, blaming my husband, opening old scars and allowing them to bleed into new wounds.

Some of the pain was avoidable: listening to Satan's whispered lies instead of God's eternal truth.

During this storming phase of my life, Satan was

hard at work. Oh, but God was hard at work too! Satan is a sneaky adversary. He hates the idea of loving families and loving homes spreading love into the world. Satan knows our weaknesses, and he specifically targets those areas. He does it in such sly ways that we often don't attribute any of the problem to him, but rather blame it on our spouses or our children.

He would "whisper" in my ear, *Scott should be doing more. Look at what he expects of you! He goes to work and gets to hang out with his friends. He probably chats in the hallways and laughs in the boardroom and has about fifteen coffee breaks before noon. Then he comes home and he doesn't even help with the dishes! Oh, that ungrateful man. If only he would offer to do more. You shouldn't have to ask him. He should know that you need his help. If he really loved you, he would take out the trash.* Satan's whispers sounded an awful lot like my own selfish thoughts. They would fill my head and have me angry at my husband before he even stepped foot in the door.

Satan would accuse, *What have you done? Look at all the drama you brought into your home. Poor Joel. Poor Hannah. You have ruined their lives. They used to have it so easy. They would be more well-adjusted, happy children if you had never adopted.* His words sounded like my own secret fears. The doubts would swirl through my head, stir up my heart, and create angst in my home.

There were too many days when those lies from Satan infected my attitude. His whispered lies mixed with my sin nature and created a lethal substance. It was so thick and dark that it blocked my view of the truth.

> Truth: God chose these children for me and me for them.
> Truth: Adoption is the right thing for our family.
> Truth: I love my husband.

In order to break down that lethal substance, in order to clean my heart and refocus my eyes and re-define what I believed *love* to mean, I had to wash myself with God's word.

> *So, chosen by God for this new life of love, dress in the wardrobe God picked out for you: compassion, kindness, humility, quiet strength, discipline. Be even-tempered, content with second place, quick to forgive an offense. Forgive as quickly and completely as the Master forgave you. And regardless of what else you put on, wear love. It's your basic, all-purpose garment. Never be without it. (Colossians 3:12–14)*

I was chosen by God for this new life of love.

> Truth: He chose me.
> Truth: He gave me a new life.
> Truth: It is a life of love.

God had picked out the perfect wardrobe for me. Compassion. Kindness. Humility. Quiet strength. Discipline. Even temperament. Contentment with second place. Quickness to forgive. Love. Sounds like the makings of a beautiful outfit. A beautiful woman. From the inside out. But I didn't feel like a beautiful woman. I didn't feel like I could fit into any of those garments anymore. "And regardless of what else you put on, wear love. It's your basic, all-purpose garment. Never be without it."

Love was meant to be my basic, all-purpose garment. Kind of like my yoga pants. Stretchy and comfortable. Love was big enough to cover up the extra pounds, the stretch marks, and the imperfections. It was warm enough to wear through the fiercest of storms.

We all have love hanging in our closet. Maybe it is pushed to the back and forgotten. Maybe it needs to be cleaned up and embroidered; the seams might need some reinforcement. But we were all given the basic, all-purpose garment of love. We just need to pull it out and get dressed.

As I tried to squeeze my old ideas into this new definition of love, I knew I would never find the perfect fit unless I spent time with the One who designed me.

I realized the first person who needed to be changed in this new definition of love was ME. That change began with consumption of the Word of

God. The only way I would be able to put on those garments and *keep* them on throughout the minutiae of this new life was by reshaping myself to look more like God.

> *I want you woven into a tapestry of love, in touch with everything there is to know of God. Then you will have minds confident and at rest, focused on Christ, God's great mystery. All the richest treasures of wisdom and knowledge are embedded in that mystery and nowhere else. (Colossians 2:2–3)*

Isn't it reassuring to know that we don't have to rely on our own love to get the job done? Our own love is imperfect at best. But we can weave our love together with the most perfect love of all. "Woven into a tapestry of love." Our families, our God, our own hearts—woven together into a tapestry of love.

During those stormy days, when every relationship and emotion in my life was being redefined, I had only one constant. One thing to rely on to fill in the cracks, to shore up the outer banks, to be the cornerstone of this new family. God's love. My love just wasn't cutting it. I needed His love to fill me up. I needed His love to pour out of me. I needed His love to be the love I offered my children when I was not feeling any love of my own.

I had a constant prayer during those days. It was

the prayer I whispered whenever I found myself empty: "Please, God, fill me up with Your love for my children. Give me Your unnatural, never-ending, unconditional, overflowing love."

Because even though I was not sure of much, I was and continue to be sure of this: God loves my children more than I could even begin to comprehend.

He answered my prayers. I felt His love emerging through my broken expectations, relationships, and heart. His love was the love I would pour out on my children.

My children were slowly learning to trust my love. They tested it. Hammered at it. Punished it. Pushed it away. And when God's love never weakened or softened, they began to believe in it.

It took a long time. We had to do life together. We had to share experiences and create memories.

Slowly, oh so very slowly, my children began responding. Maybe they would wrap their arms around me without my prompting. Maybe they would repeat "I love you" without my asking.

But I started to notice something. Something that pierces my heart and makes me catch my breath. Something that I hope I never take for granted.

My children are telling me they love me.

Not in response to my spoken words, but of their own initiative.

Naomi was the first. She is the most openly affectionate. She tested out those words for the others, and when she found them sweet on her tongue, she started using them often.

"Bye, Mom! I love you!"

"Good night, Mom. I love you."

The boys followed next. As I finish their bedtime prayers, and kiss their foreheads, and hug their little bodies close to mine, they will often be the first to say, "I love you."

And Leah. The most hesitant of all. The words have been wrestled from her tongue very sparingly. But they have come.

It took more than a year. A year of redefining love for every person in our family. A year of storming. A year of broken relationships and restoration. And then, one day, as I was serving dinner and the boys were clamoring to eat *right now*, and Naomi and Hannah were singing a new song they'd learned at school, and Scott was pouring the milk and wiping up spills, and the dog was barking to be let outside, Leah came up to me and said, "Can I tell you a secret, Mom?"

I almost kept moving. I was about to whip the potatoes and butter the broccoli. Everyone was waiting on me. I almost let the moment pass. But I stopped and bent down so she could whisper in my ear.

"Mommy, I love you so, so, so, so much. I really do love you."

Then she squeezed my neck in a quick hug and continued on her way to wash her hands.

I was left there, standing in my kitchen, holding a precious gift in my heart.

I do believe this was the first time she had spoken those words completely unprompted and unsolicited. And, true to her nature, she did it on her terms. She stored up those words, like precious jewels, until she was certain of their validity, and then she proclaimed her love in a big way, pouring out the words in bountiful measure.

May I never take these precious words for granted. May they never become background noise to my busy life. May I always take the time to stop and hear the secrets that my children are ready to whisper in my ear.

25

THE PROMISED LAND

On our first Valentine's Day when we were dating, my husband lied to me.

He was trying so hard to impress me, his new girlfriend. He had a dozen roses delivered to me at work. He picked me up in his freshly washed car. He made reservations at two different restaurants, both of which were an hour's drive away. Both were beautiful little places out in the countryside.

As he walked me to the car, he said I could choose where we went for dinner. He listed my two options.

I said, "Let's go somewhere in town. I don't want to drive so far. Did you make reservations for anyplace close by?"

He was only seventeen. Still wet behind the ears. He didn't want to disappoint his lady. So he lied.

"Yes," he said. "I made reservations for a place right down the road."

Scott obviously didn't think his plan through. Did he really imagine we could walk into a restaurant on Valentine's Day without reservations and magically be seated?

We tried. But for some reason they could not find his name on the list, and we were quickly back outside with nothing to eat.

Since then, our Valentine's Day dates have only improved. He has redeemed himself many times over. We have eaten in a tiny courtyard café surrounded by twinkle lights. In a restaurant with an open kitchen where we watched the chef prepare our meal. In a tiny farm-to-table restaurant where I tasted the very best risotto of my life. In an all-you-can-eat buffet where the overcooked chicken gave me indigestion.

Oh, wait. That last one wasn't necessarily an improvement.

But it was our first Valentine's Day with six children. We were not yet at the place in our family relationship where we could leave them with a babysitter. So we loaded up all eight of us and hit the local buffet.

The kids were in heaven. As much macaroni and cheese as they could stuff in their bellies. Unlimited soda. Dessert for everyone. A tradition was born.

We now celebrate Valentine's Day as a family. My husband and I make sure we have plenty of other romantic dinners together, but we choose to celebrate our family's love on this particular day.

We let the children choose the restaurant. Majority rules, as it is not humanly possible to make six children agree on anything.

This past Valentine's Day we found ourselves in a local steak house. We went through the ordeal of choosing everyone's meals, and the very patient waiter left with our order. Then my husband said something that made my heart explode with love.

He looked around the table at his family and said, "This is my promised land."

As he explained what he meant, my eyes filled with tears.

The Israelites had been living as slaves. You would think they'd be desperate to escape. But no. They had accepted their reality. They adjusted their expectations to be lower than what God desired for them. They were so busy living their lives, they didn't dare to dream there could be anything more.

Then God called them out. He asked them to leave behind everything they knew—and follow Him. They were scared. Venturing into the unknown is always scary. It is easier to live in the security of what you can see than to trust an invisible God.

And when you finally listen, when you obey and take that first step, when you venture out of the boat—instead of finding peace you find yourself in the middle of a storm. You doubt you're where you're supposed to be.

Though the Israelites obeyed God, they found

themselves in a desert. They had done what God had asked: They followed Him, a little begrudgingly at first, with a lot of complaining. But they followed. Only He didn't seem to be taking them into the Promised Land. Instead, He took them into the desert. A desert filled with:

- Scorching heat
- Stinging snakes
- Hunger
- Thirst
- Unrest

For forty years they lived in these conditions. They lived in the desert until they learned the lessons God needed them to learn:

- To rely on Him
- To turn to Him
- To trust in Him

Then and only then did God bring them to their Promised Land. Just as He did with our family.

He called us out of the life to which we had become accustomed. It was a good life, but He had planned something great for us. Something better. We were so busy living our lives, we had adjusted our expectations to be lower than they should have been. We could have missed out on our promised land.

I am now a different person than before God called me out. A different wife. A different mother. A different daughter. I now know my Father in different ways:

- I know He will finish what He started.
- I know He will keep His promises.
- I know He loves us so desperately, He will move mountains to draw us closer to Him.
- I know He will carry us through the desert.
- I know He will meet us in the promised land.

I look back with fondness at the woman I used to be. I kind of like her, the naive and scared soul that she was. She was struggling with control issues. (Actually, she still is.) She was fainthearted. I am proud of her for facing her fears of the unknown. She was living a good life, but she wasn't living in the fullness of the promised land.

I also look forward to the woman I'll become if I am willing to follow God toward whatever future He has planned for me. A woman of strength and wisdom. A woman who is so intertwined with her Maker, it's hard to tell where she leaves off and He begins.

I am a woman in process. We all are in process. Whether we have accepted our Egypt, are wandering through the desert, or are living in the fullness of our promised land. Our location does not determine our value. It determines only our progress.

Life won't always be filled with milk and honey. But neither will it always contain ashes and dust. There are seasons of both. The joy comes in recognizing God's presence in both places:

- Blessings in the desert
- Storms in the promised land
- God in and through it all

We spent our time wandering the desert not because God wanted us to suffer, but because He wanted us to heal. We fought our battles, we shed our tears, and we found God in that desert. We learned we had no better ally than our heavenly Father.

After we learned our lessons, after we built a faith so unshakable that earthquakes, fire, and storms could not break it apart, then God led us to our promised land. Not a place of perfection, but a place of completion.

My husband looked around the table, his eyes lingering on each of his children, then he met my gaze. He might have gotten a little misty-eyed. His voice was choked as he said, "Our family is our promised land. This is where God has been leading us all along."

26

SHUKRIYA'S PRAISE

America, 2015

Shukriya scrunched her eyes tight. The alarm was blaring on her nightstand and she heard her brothers and sisters rustling and whispering. School mornings started too early, and she wished for a few more minutes in her bed.

She could hear her sister sorting through clothes. Hannah always had a hard time choosing her outfit for the day and would often ask to borrow an article of clothing. Shukriya didn't mind. She liked being able to share clothes with both her sisters ... as long as they returned them afterward!

Shukriya could hear her mom stirring downstairs. She couldn't make out her words, but she could hear the murmur of her voice and the gurgling of the coffee machine. Her mom could be a bit grumpy before she had her coffee, but it never bothered Shukriya. Even when she was grumpy, her mom always had a hug ready for her.

Shukriya smiled as she thought about the first time she hugged her mom. She hadn't liked it much. Her body had felt stiff and unfamiliar. She had smelled different and sounded different than the people Shukriya was used to. Shukriya hugged her because that was what moms and daughters did, but it had felt like a lie.

It took a long time for those hugs to start to feel normal. Now Shukriya loved the feeling of her mom's arms wrapped around her, when she was tucked up against her mom's heart. She knew just how hard to squeeze her mom's waist. She sometimes squeezed too hard, but only because she was trying to let her mom know it no longer felt like a lie. Now it felt like love.

She could hear her little brothers arguing in the bathroom. Those two were always loud. It annoyed her sometimes because she liked it best when everyone got along. Loud voices, angry conversations, slammed doors—those bothered her more than she liked to admit. She tried her best to create peace whenever she could.

Shukriya rolled over to face the room and hit the alarm's silence button. She closed her eyes. Just a few more minutes.

In the dark and quiet of her own bed, Shukriya

breathed in deeply and felt happiness fill her insides. She liked having her own bed, sharing a room with her sister, living in this family—even though it was sometimes loud. She missed a lot of things about Ethiopia, but she loved a lot of things about America.

Being adopted was mostly a good thing, but a little bit of a bad thing. It was hard sometimes when she thought too deeply about home. She felt sad inside. She missed her mom. She missed the quiet of their little hut on the edge of the fields. She even missed the early morning walks to the river and carrying the heavy water jug.

She did not miss being hungry all the time. She didn't miss living in the orphanage.

"Thank You, Jesus, that I am not hungry anymore. Thank You for bringing my sister back to me. And thank You for my new family. Please watch over my mom today. Help her to know that I love her and miss her a lot."

Shukriya still talked to God all the time. She liked knowing He was always listening to her. He had been with her all along. He was with her in the emptiness of the locked hut. He was with her in the darkness of the lonely orphanage. And He was still with her even when she came all the way to America.

Since coming to America she had learned a lot about who God is. She now knew about His Son, Jesus. She knew He had died for her. And she knew she would meet Him someday in heaven.

Though she had not known all the details of God's story back there in Ethiopia, she had still known who He was. Way down deep inside, she had felt Him.

"Thank You, Jesus, for loving me. Thank You for loving me no matter where I am."

Shukriya knew that God had brought her to America for a reason. Though she missed a lot of things from back home, she was thankful to know God had a plan for her life. She liked to say that she came to America to meet Jesus.

Shukriya spent a lot of time thinking about heaven—a place she would get to live one day with all her family. Jesus would be there. Her Ethiopian mom would be there. And her American mom would be there. All her family would be together and living in one place. That thought made her happy.

"Thank You, Jesus, for my family. For all of my family. Watch over us all. Be with us all no matter where we go."

Then, with peace filling her heart, Shukriya opened her eyes to face a new day.

27

REDEEMED

I am writing this from my hotel room on the twentieth floor, my feet propped on a sunny windowsill, the Charles River spread out before me like a glittering smile. Brownstones line the streets, and the cherry blossoms are bright and white. It's springtime in Boston.

My husband is in a conference room somewhere below me. He has meetings all day, then tonight he will take me to dinner. I'm not sure where we will go, but I know I'll wear my black dress and my red heels. We will sit outside. We will talk and laugh and enjoy a glass of wine.

My children are back home in California. While we are gone they are staying with a variety of friends. They are in their final weeks of the school year, busy with projects and field trips. They have soccer practice and dance class and piano lessons.

And I am writing this book's final chapter, the one about redemption. My heart is overwhelmed by God's goodness. I recognize the privilege of being right here, right now, writing words like *redemption*.

My life today does not look like my life two years ago. Or four years ago.

Four years ago I was a mama to two beautiful children. We were dreaming of expanding our family through adoption. We knew our children's names, but we had never seen their faces. We knew our future would include transition, but we had no idea of the havoc that awaited us.

Two years ago I was a mama to six beautiful children. We were in the midst of the carnage. Every day was a struggle. We were fighting our way through trauma and bonding. The emotional toll was very high, and we had grown weary from the battle.

I remember a conversation with my husband during the worst of the storm. In a rare moment of uninterrupted conversation, he asked me to rate my stress level.

I started to laugh.

"Seriously," he said, "on a scale of one to ten, what is your stress level every day? Four? Five? Six?"

Then I started to cry.

Because I couldn't stop him until he reached the number nine.

We were living in a state of chaos. The tantrums.

The rages. Hitting. Angry faces twisted with venom. Nasty words thrown like arrows. Tears enough to fill an ocean.

We had to fight through a lot of pain in our children's past. We could not leave our children. There were no date nights or weekends away. I was homebound for a year as we uncovered buried trauma—one painstaking layer at a time.

There was no easy way through it. There was no going around it. There was no ignoring it. We had to wade through the middle of the whole stinking mess.

A little piece of your heart breaks when your child says, "I have never been happy. Not one time ever. I was not happy in Ethiopia. I am not happy in America. I wish I could die."

"I wish I had never been born."

"We are not a real family."

When I heard those things—when I was on the receiving end of anger that stemmed from hurts I did not cause, when I dealt with the same issue for the hundredth time, when I had to remind them again and again that they were not allowed to treat a mother like that—it was hard to respond with love. It was hard to offer forgiveness. My inner being reared up in self-righteous indignation. My heart of hearts cried out. My soul was anguished.

I messed up a lot in those early days.

Whether or not I wanted to admit it, all the battles

in my family did not originate with my children. Some arose from deep in my own soul.

My children weren't the only broken people in our family. I was just as broken. We all are just as broken. We all have trauma in our past. Maybe it's trauma with a capital *T*. Maybe with a lowercase *t*. But we all have broken pieces. We all are broken in different ways, none any better or any worse than another.

When my broken pieces rubbed against my children's broken pieces, it was easy for someone to get hurt.

Of course, this applies to all our relationships. We live in a broken world, full of broken people. We can easily let this translate into broken relationships.

Or we can fight to persevere and work to mend and heal our relationships.

The only way to do this is by recognizing our own broken places. That's the only road to true healing. Until we admit our own weaknesses, we can't become stronger.

I had to admit my pride. I had to deal with my selfishness. I had to face my sin. I had to relinquish my desire for control.

Only then could God bring full restoration to every member of my family. God took all those broken pieces and fitted them together to create something beautiful. He fulfilled the promise He made in Colossians: "All the broken and dislocated pieces of the universe—people and things, animals and atoms—get properly fixed and fit together in vibrant harmonies, all because of his death, his blood that poured down from the Cross" (1:20).

It did not happen overnight. It took time. Anything strong and lasting takes time to build. If you're under construction, don't give up. It might not be today, it probably won't be tomorrow, but restoration for you is coming.

Redemption is coming.

Redemption does not mean "perfection." My family is far from perfect. I wouldn't even call my family normal. I don't expect we'll ever be normal. We will always look different, love differently, and live differently.

But however it appears, redemption is gloriously beautiful. It's messy and far from normal—and I wouldn't have it any other way.

For you, redemption might look like a restored relationship. Maybe it could be found in asking for or offering forgiveness. Maybe it's in finally forgiving yourself. Maybe in picking up the phone, taking the first step, reaching out your hand. Often people find redemption in letting go: of expectations, of requirements, of control.

Frequently, redemption looks like love. Loving with no strings attached. Loving without any rules. Loving big and hard and boldly. Redemption is a very personal thing, so it looks different for each of us.

This is what redemption looks like for me.

Redemption looks like dinner on the back patio. We still haven't gotten a new outdoor table, so we somehow squeeze all eight of us around the old one, pulling extra chairs from wherever we can find them. We bump elbows and reach over one another as we eat. Someone spills their milk, but it doesn't matter because the puppy will lick it up. I can't hear my husband because everyone is always talking at the same time. It's loud, and the mosquitoes are thick, so it's itchy. The citronella candles are flickering and the laughter is flowing. It looks like chaos.

Redemption looks like too much homework. Science fair and school projects and spelling words. My oldest son helping my youngest with his math facts. My daughter is worrying about her history test. Trying to squeeze in the book report between dinner and soccer practice. It looks like busyness.

Redemption looks like bedtime prayers and extra snuggles. A schedule for bath nights so we don't run out of hot water. Night-lights in the little boys' room because they are afraid of the dark. Talking quietly with my girls in their darkened bedrooms about this and that and everything and nothing. Tiptoeing through the sleeping house, pulling up covers and smoothing down curls. It looks like tiredness.

Redemption looks like phone calls home. Late at night in California, early morning in Ethiopia, a static-filled connection drawing us toward each other. We dial. She answers and her voice fills the space between us. Words come haltingly and sometimes uncomfortably as we navigate these rocky relationships. Some children press in closer, some pull away. It looks like confusion.

Redemption looks like ongoing counseling sessions. Sharing our innermost fears with one another and with Miss Colleen. Horse-riding therapy and music therapy and for me the occasional glass-of-wine-while-I-cry-with-my-girlfriends therapy. Refusing to allow our feelings to be our boss and instead using those feelings to sew a stronger family fabric. It looks like connectedness.

Redemption looks like springtime in Boston: my husband attending business meetings, me writing in the quiet of a hotel room. Dinner tonight on an outdoor patio. Holding hands. Talking softly. A marriage that's stronger because of the trials we've faced together. It looks like love.

Redemption looks like eight imperfect people who together form a family more glorious than I'd dared to dream of. It looks like us.

ACKNOWLEDGMENTS

On a cool October evening in 2015 I sat around a fire pit with seven women. They were my confidantes, cheerleaders, and friends. Someone posed the question: What is your *one thing*? The one dream you would chase if nothing was holding you back? I said I wanted to write a book. This was the first time I'd spoken my dream out loud to anyone other than my husband. My girlfriends adopted my dream as their own. They nurtured it, spoke life into it, and prayed over it. If it weren't for these women, this book might still be hiding in my soul: Kara Ayer, Gina Basham, Brenda Clark, LynneAnne Dewitt, Jessica Matos, Faith McCarthy, and Deborah Skinner.

Amanda Crawford-Basaraba and Katie McManus, you make long-distance friendship seem easy. Thank you for being text encouragers extraordinaire.

Ellen Pfeiffer, you believed in me from the very beginning. You made me believe in myself.

Thank you to my pastor, Bill Giovannetti, for speaking truth from the pulpit every Sunday, for critiquing my first rambling chapters and for introducing me to my agent. I owe you a Lou Malnati's pizza.

To my agent, Janet Grant, I know I didn't follow any of the rules on the road to publication. Thank you for throwing the rule book out the window and representing me anyway.

Thank you to my editor, Adrienne Ingrum. I don't know why you decided to take a chance on a newbie like me, but I couldn't be more grateful. You championed my work from the beginning and have been a dream to collaborate with every step of the way. I want to make you proud.

My children, Joel, Leah, Naomi, Hannah, Micah, and Levi. You are everything I never knew I always wanted. I think I've heard that phrase somewhere before, but it is exactly how I feel about all of you. I thank God daily for turning my life upside down and giving me more than I deserve. I love you.

And to my husband. My feelings for you are too big to be contained in these words. You are my champion, my supporter, my best friend. You were the first to say we should start dating, the first to bring up the idea of marriage, the first to suggest having a baby, the first to mention adoption, the first to tell me I should write a book. You are the beginning of all the best things in my life. I will love you always and forever.

ABOUT THE AUTHOR

Natalie Gwyn lives in Northern California with her high school sweetheart. Together they are raising six beautiful children. Natalie excels at laundry and laughter. She struggles mightily with patience and all things crafty. In between sorting socks and driving car pool, she writes for *Huffington Post*, *Today*, and *Guideposts*. She blogs about family, friendship, fitness, and faith on her website, nataliegwyn.com.

THE AUTHOR IS PROUD TO SUPPORT LIFESONG FOR ORPHANS!

Lifesong for Orphans is dedicated to bringing joy and purpose to orphans and vulnerable children through family preservation, adoption funding, global orphan care, and foster care support. By mobilizing advocates, families, and churches, Lifesong serves children and caregivers worldwide.

Specifically, Lifesong children will

- not want for food, clothing, medical care, or shelter
- be taught the Gospel and how to live as followers of Christ
- receive a quality education to provide a foundation for their future
- experience continued love and support as they transition into adult living

Thanks to TMG Foundation and key partners, all of Lifesong's fund-raising and administrative costs are already covered, meaning 100 percent of received donations will directly help children in need.

www.lifesongfororphans.org
P.O. Box 40
Gridley, IL 61744
309-747-4527

31901063439634